# LETTERS
### AND
## REMINISCENCES
#### OF
# EMILY BORLASE BOLITHO.

---

*PORTRAIT, 1885.*

---

PENZANCE:
BEARE & SON, 21, MARKET PLACE.
1889.

This scarce antiquarian book is included in our special *Legacy Reprint Series*. In the interest of creating a more extensive selection of rare historical book reprints, we have chosen to reproduce this title even though it may possibly have occasional imperfections such as missing and blurred pages, missing text, poor pictures, markings, dark backgrounds and other reproduction issues beyond our control. Because this work is culturally important, we have made it available as a part of our commitment to protecting, preserving and promoting the world's literature. Thank you for your understanding.

## *PREFACE.*

DISAPPOINTMENT will, we fear, be the prevailing feeling of Emily Bolitho's old friends on reading these pages. The letters are not sufficiently varied or representative; they give but a faint idea of her most charming traits; they form a very imperfect chronicle of her life, and the void is in no way filled by the meagre sketch accompanying them.

In apology we would explain briefly that the great mass of her most important letters has, unfortunately, not been preserved; that it is only by repeated efforts on the part of kind friends that any have been collected.

Most grateful thanks are due to all those who have so courteously helped, either by allowing selections to be made from their letters, or by kindly furnishing reminiscences of their intercourse with her.

One word on the want of variety in the letters; beyond their direct spiritual teaching the chief characteristic shown in them is her loving, anxious interest in every detail of the lives of all she loved; many seemingly trivial sentences which would otherwise have been omitted have been left intact because exemplifying this; as regards the absence of that wit and originality with which her conversation overflowed, it must be borne in mind that her great power undoubtedly lay in speech rather than in writing, and that both her particular line of work and her daily family intercourse constantly developed the

## PREFACE.

former, while giving her little opportunity of studying the latter. Her letters as a rule were written very hastily (generally late at night), without any thought as to composition; simple outpourings of religious fervour or tender sympathy, coming straight from her heart. She would have shrunk in all humility from the thought of their being made public; though if convinced of their power to convey spiritual help, we feel assured that her consent would have been given, for as we are told of another saintly woman, " whenever she felt the story of God's dealings in her own life could lead others to a simpler faith and more entire trust in Him, she never allowed any self-seeking reticence to interfere with this instrumentality."

We humbly trust that this little volume, with all its imperfections, may yet fulfil two purposes:—first, of extending her good example and influence to those who never knew Emily Bolitho in the flesh; secondly, of recalling to those who had that privilege many more important words of hers, and so keeping her teaching fresh in their minds. If this be so, the unworthiness of the connecting thread will perhaps be overlooked; the roughness of the strand pass unheeded for the sake of the pearls which it saves from being scattered and lost in the dust of oblivion.

E. B.

Penzance, *St. Andrew's Day, 1889.*

# CONTENTS.

## CHAPTER I.

### (1817—1854.)

Birth—Childhood—Letter from Miss F. Grenfell—School-days—Letters from Miss E. Carne—Home-life—Visit to Pendeen . . . . 1

## CHAPTER II.

### (1854—1882.)

### LETTERS TO AND FROM REV. R. AND MRS. AITKEN.

First visit to Pendeen—Conversion—Anxiety for spiritual growth—Letter from Mr. Haslam—Birthdays, 1854-55—Rev. G. Fenton's coming to St. Paul's, Penzance, 1856—Extracts about Father's death, 1857-58—Lizzie Marks—Anniversary of first visit to Pendeen—All Saints' Day—Mr. Aitken's birthday—Captain Bedford's death, 1868—Ascension Day, 1868—Death of Mrs. Aitken's grandchild, 1868—Christmas, 1869—Mr. Aitken's birthday, 1870—Mr. Grant's death, 1870—Ascension Day, 1870—Mrs. Aitken's sister's death, 1872—Birthday, 1877—Remembrance of Mr. Aitken's Birthday, 1880—Conversion of old servant, 1882 . . . . . . . . . . . 21

## CONTENTS.

### CHAPTER III.
#### (1869—1884.)
#### *LETTERS TO FRIENDS.*

To Miss Powell, on Consecration of St. Paul's—On Captain Bedford's death—Easter, 1869, Rev. A. Mills's sermon—Watch-night Service, 1872—Death of Louie Wright—Rev. R. Aitken's death and funeral—Confirmation at Penzance—Christmas—Letters to Mr. Elwin—To Rev. G. Fenton—To Miss Fenton—To Rev. G. Savage—To Miss Haydon—To Miss M. E. Tregelles—To Miss Emma Stevens—To Miss M. Tyacke, on death of Lizzie Marks . . . . . 64

### CHAPTER IV.
#### 1859—1885.)
#### *FAMILY LETTERS.*

To a niece, on spiritual difficulties—To a Goddaughter, on her Confirmation—To her niece Mrs. Foster, on "Sister Dora;" on Rev. W. H. Aitken's Mission at Penzance, 1879; on Birthday; on Moody and Sankey's Mission at Plymouth, 1882; New Year's Greetings; Illness of old servant; Meeting Bishop at Pendeen; Easter, 1885—To a sister, on her daughter's death—To her niece Mrs. John Bolitho, on sad anniversaries—To her great-niece Ruth, for Christmas . . . . 115

### CHAPTER V.
#### *REMINISCENCES.*

Letters from friends:—Prebendary Hedgeland, Rev. R. W. Aitken, Rev. W. Hay Aitken, Rev. R. J. Martyn, Rev. R. J. Roe, Miss M. Tyacke, Miss J. Moyle, Miss Haydon, Miss M. Tregelles, Mrs. Cay, Miss Anna Maria Fox, Mrs. Herbert, Miss Mary Rogers, Sister Anna, Rev. A. L. Palmes—Extracts from Diary—Visits to Lanwithan—To Trevaylor to meet the Bishop—Last Letter—Illness—Death . . . . . 139

# Letters and Reminiscences

OF

# EMILY BORLASE BOLITHO.

## CHAPTER I.

(1817-54.)

Birth—Childhood—Letter from Miss F. Grenfell—School-days—Letters from Miss E. Carne—Home-life—Visit to Pendeen.

"WE want the biographies of common people," Froude says; and, commenting on this, another writer adds, "They may be uneventful and uninteresting lives, lived out in some quiet corner in monotony, in common-place duties . . . . with narrow means perhaps, and little leisure or opportunity of culture; but in spite of all this, and beyond and breaking through all this, are yet beautiful in their example, golden in their teaching, and kindling by their animating power."

Such was she of whom we are attempting this short sketch: we find no stirring events, no great outward changes in the even course of her life.

Emily Borlase Bolitho was the fifth daughter of Thomas and Maria Bolitho, of the Coombe, Penzance. She was born on

October 11th, 1817, and lived all her busy and useful days in her birthplace, and there she died; her absences were never longer than for a few months, so that there is little variety to form an extended narrative. All her many friends will remember fondly, without need of description, the comfortable, old-fashioned granite-fronted house, with its windows down to the ground opening on to the little lawn, shut off by shrubs from the road, and with a charming peep of the sea over the wicket gate at the bottom; they will remember, too, the delightful old garden— half flower, half vegetable—on the side of the hill, with the "red river," as the tin-stained stream was called, flowing through it; the earliest of spring nosegays were always to be gathered there, and the sweetest of old-fashioned roses and other summer flowers not only brightened her own rooms, but those of many poor and sick for whom they were liberally cut. To many no doubt the Coombe was endeared by happy memories of past family gatherings; to others only by her own genial presence and hearty welcome; but to all, whether relatives, long-standing friends, or casual visitors, the peaceful old-world home seemed invested with a peculiar charm.

The house is situated only a few yards from the shore, with a glimpse of the beautiful eastern sweep of Mount's Bay, but immediately outside the gate stand the buildings connected with her family's tin-smelting works, and their offices of business. The din and stir of constant traffic must have mingled from her earliest recollections with the more musical sound of the waves breaking on the beach below. Her character seemed to take the impress of her home: as there the active and practical combined with the beautiful and poetic, so her mind appeared to comprise both these elements; even when most carried away by her religious enthusiasm she always retained her hereditary clear judgment and strong common-sense. "She was," a poor woman once said of her, "so good for this world, as well as for the next."

Much, too, that was beautiful in her character may be traced to the bringing up in that full, happy home. The fifth girl in a family of six daughters and three sons, she seems to have had a very free, joyous childhood, and yet to have recognised a discipline indispensable to the sound moral training of that large family. She used often to say that her mother was a woman of very few words, but that her word was always law; that if any hesitation was shown in at once complying, she would say in a tone they feared above all things, "If you do that again, you and I shall differ," and none of them had ever ventured to put to the proof this ominous threat.

Perhaps the best picture of the Coombe home-life in her early days is this drawn by a great friend and contemporary, Miss Fanny Grenfell:—

". . . . You know we were quite little girls when we first met, and I well remember her figure and her bright little face that morning, when she appeared at the window of the Coombe dining-room in her garden dress, having been hastily called in to see me, as I accompanied some one or other (who it was, I cannot recollect, but probably my dear father).

"Dear Emily was as plump and comfortable a little child of six or seven as *I* was, I expect, the contrary; and she had an immense nosegay of lovely primroses just gathered which she at once thrust into my tiny hand with a hearty kiss, and *possessing* herself of the little shy plain child a year older than herself she then and there made friends, and that friendship grew and strengthened for many a long year, in spite of the contrast we presented to each other in many ways; but, of course, full of strength and spirits as she was, and bred up in such a free and wholesome family atmosphere (as her dear mother's house presented to my mind), there could be no doubt as to who took the lead, and she was usually followed willingly; also her will at that time was the strongest.

"We might do as we chose at the Coombe, if only we did nothing thought wrong; run about in most delightful round pinafores—get pails of water and wash all the empty pots in the greenhouse in the further kitchen garden, or in the 'red river' —play at cottage-folk in the tiny arbour—or, better still, followed perhaps by 'little Kate' and another, and (when lucky enough to get him) my brother Henry, who was a great chum of dear Emily's, run right through the river leading down to the sea at Chyandour, if the stream ran nearly dry so as not to hurt us. Usually old Tammie, the nurse, rated us on our return.

"The Coombe was 'Liberty Hall,' and the delights to us so varied that I used to scheme with her to get sent to bed at the same time with herself, if, when having spent a long day there, our servant did not appear to take us in reasonable time, and it happened to rain a little. I am sorry to say that on one occasion we were, as we trusted, safely lodged together for the night, when a peremptory summons home, in the shape of two inexorable maids, appeared, and go we must! Oh, misery! imagine the scuffle! for my dear kind father never could bear us to be away for one night. Emily was *always* a favorite with him for her unfailing good humour, her handsome face, etc., and of course the visits were returned.

"She was never a *grave* girl you know, so I did not often succeed, as time went on, in getting her to join heartily in any *book* pleasure; she had " other fish to fry," and I fear at one time was rather frivolously disposed, but she was ever *true*, unselfish, and sympathizing; and on our returns from our several schools she used to fly to meet and embrace me warmly, and we often exchanged confidences as to our experiences at school, our scrapes, etc., etc., and being naughty sometimes of course. She was always greatly beloved by school-fellows, nurses and servants, and all inferiors; her generous disposition was early apparent.

"And now, alas! I know but little of her life after adversity on my side parted us. I know that we parted with many tears, never expecting to meet again, *for the doctors doomed me to an early death*, much they knew what God meant to do with us; and here I am, sixty-nine years of age, having weathered a lifetime of varied maladies, and allowed to live when no one wants me, and *Emily*, the centre almost of a large circle of relations, devoted friends—many young, and poor and suffering in numbers to lament her loss and help in every way, is cut off like a shock of corn fully ripe, leaving a blessed memory behind her of good deeds done, from a loving heart, to her Saviour and His children; as far as I know every relative duty performed strictly, many souls helped, as I believe, though I am a Catholic; and yet her favorite words were, when I remember her last in 1861 (or '62, I do not exactly recollect),

'I'm a poor sinner, and nothing at all,
But *Jesus Christ* is my All in All.'

And I believe she is *with Him*, which is much for a Catholic to say; but on that subject I need not speak. 'Faithful unto death,' I believe she gained the 'Crown of Life.'

"Her happy spirit! may I one day meet her, my dear old friend! . . . . . ."

From this charming sketch of Emily Bolitho's childhood we turn to almost the only great break in her life at the Coombe, her being sent away to school at Mrs. Grenfell's, at Tor, in 1831. We do not find that she ever distinguished herself in her studies; in fact, from her own account she was often in disgrace, not from real naughtiness, but from her high spirits and love of fun, and perhaps impatience of the irksome restraints of a school, which, contrasted with her former freedom of life, must have been peculiarly trying to one of her impetuous, active temperament. We should mention that before being sent to Tor her education had been begun at a day-school in Penzance. Of this time another friend writes: "When we all went to school together at Miss Cox's, in 1825, I remember her as an odd, impulsive, affectionate child, but I cannot then remember anything of the quaint originality which was so delightful in later years."

Judging by a few scraps found among her papers, it seems that when at Mrs. Grenfell's her hasty tongue was sometimes led into slips of grammar or slang expressions, which apparently she had to pay the penalty of writing out,—first her own incorrect speech, and then her governess's somewhat stiff improvement:—

| *Said.* | *Corrected.* |
|---|---|
| I have to go on with my French in such a rattle-cum-chase if Fanny is before. | When Fanny is before me, I am obliged to hurry on with my French. |
| Mamma and Papa think them the wrongest things possible. | Mamma and Papa think them very injurious. |
| I do not like to see the writing lop-sided, Miss Eleanor. | I do not like to see the writing uneven, Miss Eleanor. |

"Miss Eleanor" was Mrs. Grenfell's younger daughter, and we are told that "the serious impressions Emily Bolitho had had when very young were strengthened when at school by the loving advice and prayers of this governess, whom she loved dearly."

The following exercise letter to her school-mistress shows that she had already good powers of description, and was a keen and intelligent observer:—

### *Emily Bolitho to her School-mistress.*

*October 2nd, 1833.*

My dear Mrs. Grenfell,—As you wished me to give you an account of what we saw in our last excursion, I will now do so. The trees in the avenues are ash, oak, elm, sycamore, beech, and maple, most of which are very fine. There were several deer lying down in groups, which looked very happy in each other's company; the spotted are very handsome. There is a pretty brook with three boats and two boat-houses; all along the water trees are planted. The house is large, but we were not near enough to see of what stone it is built.

On leaving the park[1] we came to Chudleigh; a great part of the town was destroyed some years since by fire. The drive from the school to the rocks is extremely pretty; the country is beautifully wooded.

As there had been so much rain, we were obliged to dine in the carriage, on the step of which Miss Rogers sat as queen, with her brothers at her feet. After dinner we went on our way to the rocks through a coppice, in which there were a great number of small oak trees.

[1] Ugbrooke Park.

We were so long at dinner that it was time to return before we could reach the rocks, which are composed of blueish limestone. Chudleigh is famed for its woollen manufactories. . . . . I am sorry that I cannot give you a better account of what I saw. I must now thank you for forming so delightful a party for us, and
Believe me to remain, my dear Mrs. Grenfell,
Your very affectionate and dutiful pupil,
E. B. BOLITHO.

Though often led away by her high spirits and love of fun she never forgot the religious teaching of her early childhood, and even fifty years after would recall instances of how her conscience had been touched by different occurrences. One was, that she and another girl, both often in disgrace for smiling or giggling in church, once dressed themselves in double thick veils, arranged in such a way they imagined as to conceal their faces entirely. The preacher chose for his text, "Be sure your sin will find you out," and Emily Bolitho felt it as if directed specially at her, and throughout the sermon was in an agony of shame and sorrow.

Her confirmation took place at home,[1] and made such a solemn and deep impression on her, she used to say, that on seeing the Bishop and others driving off afterwards to a Geological Meeting, she exclaimed, "Oh how *can* they!" because to her it seemed too sacred a day for any occupation but prayer.

She left school at Christmas, 1833, when about seventeen, in bad health, a victim, like many girls of that age, to hysteria; but this seems to have soon passed off, and we find her settling into a busy, active home-life; her time divided between the claims of her numerous relatives and those of the sick and needy in

In 1836.

the surrounding village of Chyandour, where she often taught in a school founded by her eldest sister.

She does not, however, now appear to have been of a studious turn any more than in her school-days; we are told she was rather romantic and susceptible, sociable and fond of conversation; full of a ready sympathy which made her a good listener, with a quickness of wit and keen sense of humour which always made her an attractive talker.

Her eldest brother had married in 1830, and in the course of the next ten or twelve years her second brother and her second and fourth sisters married and settled in or near Penzance, while her third sister, Maria, became the wife of the Rev. F. Gregory, Vicar of Mullion.

Though she used laughingly to say, "she had fallen in love dozens of times," and had various admirers, she never became engaged to any one. She formed at different times very strong attachments to girl-friends, notably to a Miss Letitia Carey and a Miss Gladstone. She also kept up a most friendly, affectionate intercourse with the daughters of the late Mr. Joseph Carne, of Penzance.

The following letters from Miss Elizabeth Carne, besides bearing marks of her own great intellectual ability, throw valuable light on Emily Bolitho's tone of mind, character, and occupation at this period:—

### *Miss E. T. Carne to Emily Bolitho.*

Penzance, *August 3rd, 1843.*

My dear Emily,—To write a letter to you is a most meritorious action, for who ever does it must do it without having any prospect of compensation. If you have one bad quality, it is that you are rather more fond of receiving than answering letters, as I know to my cost. Is this not the third time I have written to you? and not a line shall I see in return, with the exception of that you wrote from Cheltenham. I saw Kate in Church on Sunday week, and she told me she had left you pretty well, but I have not seen her since to hear any particulars of your movements. She told Caroline you gave her a message for me, but whether it was anything more than your direction, and a request to write, I do not know.

What are you doing with yourself, away so long? If you wish to be at the Coombe again half as much as I did to be at Penzance, I am sorry for you; but then you are with friends enjoying yourself, while we were working like horses, which makes a great difference. And then you can command quiet time and quiet thought, while we were either occupied by continued physical exertion, or inclined to lounge away time on a sofa from the effects of it. But I should like to know what your opinion is of the effects of travelling,—is it bad, or good? does it do most harm, or good? Indirectly, I think it often does good by improving health and increasing energy, and thus making one more fit to perform home duties; but on the other hand, it is sadly dissipating, at least, I find it so.

To attempt to send you any town news, when you have such excellent correspondents at Chyandour, would be superfluous trouble, but as it is just possible they may not have written since yesterday, I will venture on one piece of news. There was a regatta yesterday, and James Pascoe's boat, crowding all sail to beat Mr. Gale's, was caught by a squall, upset, filled, and went down with four men in her. Happily the cutter was near enough to send boats and pick up the men, so there were no lives lost. We have company with us at present in the shape of Dr. Johnston and his father, who left Edinburgh for a little tour in

England, and have come on stage by stage till they find themselves at Penzance, while Anna is all alone at Edinburgh. I believe you talk of the distance between yourself and Mrs. Gregory as though it were too far, but if I could but settle my sisters at Plymouth or Bath, I should think them near enough to be quite contented. I should not like to be as you are, all in the same town; it would make me feel, far more than I do at present, how great a separation their marriage had made between us, for there are a hundred little things which I should often like to tell my sisters, without exactly wishing them to be repeated to their husbands. Now many of these trifles are not worth putting in a letter; whereas if my sisters lived in the same town, I should wish to tell them, and not dare to. Besides, I would not for the world be as you are, exposed to constant interruptions from all your nearest relations and friends, with hardly an hour in the day which you can certainly call your own. In such a desultory mode of life, how is it possible to preserve any steadiness of purpose or action? and without this how little is to be done either great or good? Besides, it brings a continual feeling of self-reproach,—a sort of dissatisfaction with one's self and each ill-spent day, and the circumstances that make it so. I have often felt it myself, and I do believe it is (in a great measure) the cause of that perpetual uneasiness and self-reproach of which I have heard you complain. Your judgment leads you one way, while habit and circumstances draw you the other; you wish to have more settled pursuits, while the difficulty of making them for yourself discourages or stifles your efforts, and so you go on wishing to alter, and dissatisfied with yourself, yet never altering. I have scarcely ever had a chat with you or Kate without receiving this impression. If it is a wrong one, I heartily beg your pardon; but if I should chance to be right, do you not think your return home after such a long absence (long enough at least to break up old habits) would be an excellent time to think about forming new ones? Oh! how I do wish you would find or make a little time every day for reading (not religious reading, for I know you do that already); you know, I think it has much more to do with religion than many people at first sight imagine; it helps to control the thoughts and discipline the imagination, and this of itself is no trifling service. But it is useless to say anything more on the subject, for I am afraid you are incorrigible. That poor little book of Abercrombie's! I wonder has it ever been read through yet? I only wish Chapel street were nearer the Coombe, for if it were I would so tease you about it, that in self-defence you would begin; but certainly it is a most unfortunate distance. They say that where there is a will there is a way; but it is not always true, for the same difficulty you used to find with regard to Chyandour; the walk alone there and back takes three-quarters of an hour, and then one never thinks of going such a distance except to sit a little while and have a chat, and this with dressing and loitering will be an hour-and-half at least,—time which cannot always be spared, when half-an-hour easily might be. We find this already with regard to the B——'s. In London we were quite intimate, and saw each other continually, but here, though quite as willing, we find there are other employments to occupy us, and other friends to be seen, and P—— is such an awful distance, that in spite of the best intentions to the contrary, I fear our intimacy will relapse into our old stiff acquaintanceship. This makes me look back with respect and admiration to the days of Jack the Giant Killer; true we have railroads now, but he had seven-league boots.

If you leave London without exacting from the Braithwaites a solemn promise to spend the next winter in Penzance, none of their friends here will ever forgive you. In such a case, I have some curiosity to know whether our attempts at intimacy would die such a natural death as they did last winter. Never was there more fruitless trouble: how many calls paid and cards wasted in vain! Pray remember us to them.

I shall like to know when we meet whether you are still as dreadfully afraid of Mr. Braithwaite as formerly? In one respect you have been more fortunate than we were. Out of six sermons we heard in London, one was a dry discourse on the Trinity, and another nothing particular in any way; of the others, two from Baptist Noel were wholly controversial, and two were concluded by long controversial digressions. I should like to ascertain from the Braithwaites whether this predominance of controversy is prevalent, or merely accidental; for if prevalent, alas! for the usefulness of the Christian ministry. I do not believe any one was ever turned from sin by the most cogent arguments against Puseyism.

You will be home, I suppose, in two or three weeks,—so until then, good-bye. Anna sends her love, and she wants to see you home again. I hope to see you quite well and strong; and oh, how much there will be to tell and hear!

With kind love, believe me, my dear Emily,

Yours affectionately,

E. T. CARNE.

Top of the Faulhorn, *July 3rd, 1844.*

My dear Emily,—On the top of a mountain nine thousand feet high, where we are now snowed up, and unable to descend, with no books, no companions, no work,—in short, with nothing whatever to do but to twirl our thumbs, and keep ourselves warm, I now endeavour to fulfil my long-delayed promise by beginning a letter to you. It ought, undoubtedly, to begin with an apology for having allowed more than five weeks to pass away without finding or making an opportunity of writing, but we have only been twice stationary since leaving Penzance, and then I have had more imperative correspondents to satisfy. My fault in this case is its own punishment, as I shall be obliged to go without the answer you promised to send me, as letters take seven or eight days on the road, and I cannot send you a direction which will find me nearly three weeks from the present time, as I hope then to be turning my steps homewards under the Punnetts' care. I am very glad there is a prospect of their coming to Switzerland, or I should have been greatly at a loss for an escort home, since I find from Caroline there is little chance of the B——'s being at home before September, and that would not have suited me at all, as I wish much to return the first week in August to welcome my sister Mary and her children. I hope, if it please God, to return quite well and strong, for I am already very much better; indeed I should not know there was anything the matter with me, if I did not feel unwilling to return and undertake home duties again, which is always a sure sign with me that I need a longer absence. I am ashamed to send you such an egotistical letter as this must be, but I have really nothing to write about but my own personal concerns, and I do not suppose you would care for a dissertation on the scenery of Switzerland.

I ought to thank you for the book and note I received in the coach the morning we left Penzance. I have begun "Bickersteth" (that is all I can say, having only just begun it), and like it exceedingly. I have always felt the defect of my prayers to be, that they are more like passing wishes breathed to the air than real petitions offered to One who has promised to hear and answer them. I do not realize in prayer the presence of God, and that always makes them cold and lifeless. I hardly know if you will recollect what you said in your note—it seems so long ago, but you asked me if I ever felt a wish to pray with those I loved. No, I never did. To pray *for* them I can well understand, or even to pray *with* them, so far as to enjoy the same time and form of prayers when separate; but to kneel beside them and speak aloud my petitions to God,—no, I do not think I ever could do this to any earthly being. Do you really mean to say you have often done this, and enjoyed it? and more astonishing still that Letitia C—— has done it? I am far more surprised, knowing her timid disposition, that she should ever have done it, than that she should now decline doing it. It is, I think, a most valuable gift, especially to those who visit the poor and sick; one which I am much inclined to envy you, it is so entirely foreign to my natural disposition.

I might repeat all I said to you last summer of the unsettling effects of travelling from my own experience. My comfort is, that as I have done what I believe to be right in leaving home, all the disadvantages will be overruled for good. How much I often wish I could claim the promise that "'all things shall work together for good," but then it is only promised to them that love God. I begin to think our summer intimacy is nearly over for this season, 'tis almost like a flower that dies back every winter and shoots again in the spring. While Mary and her children are with us my time will rarely be at my own disposal, and with October comes change of weather and chilly evenings, when I cannot walk down to the Coombe to spend a sociable evening as I used to do.

Do you recollect saying in one of our tête-á-têtes how strange it was we had never known each other till lately? I quite agree there; but I do not think we know each other fully yet, at least I have sometimes thought you are hardly aware of a great difference in our dispositions, which must interfere with any closeness, or rather, I should say, with any tenderness of intimacy. All my family have a certain coldness of disposition, which is our misfortune; we cannot help it, but it causes, in general, a most unamiable and unpopular indifference to all the usual modes of showing affection. Now I see plainly, my dear Emily, these are the very things you particularly like in a friend. I have seen it more of late; for until the last twelve months we have never been on terms to allow of any degree of fondness in our intimacy, and I feel my own unfitness to please your taste in this respect. You complimented me once on being so much more gentle than I used to be, but the family disposition still remains,—improved perhaps, but I am afraid not capable of much further improvement; unless, then, you can be content to make allowance for this natural fault of character, I feel our present intimacy must come to an end, for you will think better of me, and expect more from me, than I deserve you should think or expect. I am not (I do not say it to be contradicted, but in sober earnest), I am not at all what you would call a *loveable* person, and I cannot help it. I can neither feel nor feign tenderness for many for whom I feel, and ever wish to feel, most cordial regard and esteem. I have often wished to make you understand this, but it is an awkward thing to say, and I gladly take the opportunity a letter gives me, for I know how certain a chill it gives to any intercourse to meet with coldness on either side, especially to those who, like yourself, prefer a friend whom they can fondle or caress. So I hope you will make allowance for me, dear Emily, and not expect me to be too *loveable*, which is not natural to me. I like our present cordial, unreserved intercourse, and should be sorry if any misunderstanding put an end to it, but my common manner is not a soft or tender one, which I know you prefer. I will say nothing more on this subject, for it is not at all a pleasant one. I hope when we meet it will be as kindly and cordially as we parted; until then, good-bye.

In little more than four weeks I expect to see dear old Penzance again, for by that time I shall be very glad to return, and I hope to find the Coombe less of an hospital than it was when we parted, and that you have not been staying with Mrs. Borlase again, knocking yourself up. When next you write to Letitia would you send her the enclosed; it was too little to send her by post, and as it does not increase your postage I thought you would kindly forward it for me.

A pretty affair this seems to have been between Charlotte Carey and John Richards. I think George Simmons ought to have horse-whipped him; I would, had I married Kate. Pray remember me very kindly to your circle, and with love to yourself,

   Believe me, dear Emily,
     Yours affectionately,
       E. T. CARNE.

In November, 1844, Mary Bolitho, the eldest sister, died. She had always been the moving spirit in the family; extremely kind-hearted, and a woman of very sound judgment. A friend says of her: "She was a lovely Christian character, an example of consistency to all who knew her;" and her loss was deeply felt by all. The mother never recovered the blow, and the youngest sister Kate was for the time so prostrated by it that she was sent to Leamington for three months to be under a noted doctor. Here Emily nursed and cared for her with the greatest kindness. During their stay they made the acquaintance of Miss

Gladstone, who in after years became their dearest friend, often staying for months together at the Coombe.

Family cares seem now to have increased. Mr. Gregory died in 1852, and it was Emily's part to go to Mullion and help and support her sister during his illness and death, and subsequently to arrange for the family's removal to The Abbey, Penzance. Her sister Kate married in the year 1848, so that the charge of both parents—the mother now in failing health—devolved upon Emily; and the marriage of her youngest brother in 1851 left her their sole remaining child in the once crowded home. But though no longer under the same roof, the various marriages had not taken any of them to live beyond reach of daily visits or communication. Many little ones too were growing up in the different homes, and Emily soon developed into the typical maiden-aunt. Naturally fond of children, she was devoted to those of her brothers and sisters; ever bright and affectionate, entering into all their childish games and fun with the greatest zest, and always ready with an inexhaustible stock of stories and jokes for them. And this loving sympathy grew with their growth, and strengthened with their strength, until, as the filial anxieties now occupying her were removed by death, many of these nephews and nieces as they became men and women would come to her in all their sorrows and difficulties, their joys and hopes. She became the confidante of their love-affairs, and their great counsellor in religious perplexities; and as one by one they settled in life, she extended the same large-hearted sympathy to those whom they married, so that on all sides these children of her love and prayers "rise up and call her blessed." The very title of "Aunt Emily" seemed so to establish a claim on her love, that it was in her later years generally adopted by her intimate friends.

Of her loving, unremitting care of both father and mother we need not speak; we must now refer to what she herself always looked on as the greatest turning-point in her spiritual life.

Most people in the neighbourhood of Penzance will remember or have heard of Mr. Aitken, vicar of Pendeen;—his strong, decided views on conversion; his stirring preaching and his wonderful influence, not only in awakening souls, but also in "building them up in the faith."

He did not hesitate to denounce sin and apathy in the plainest terms from the pulpit, sometimes with individual applications. His teaching caused a great sensation; some regarding it with fear and mistrust, others accepting it with the deepest enthusiasm. Among the latter was Emily Bolitho.

Up to the time of her mother's death, 1853, though sincerely religious, she had not found, she said, that "peace in believing" which she afterwards enjoyed. Some friends seeing her occasionally troubled with doubts and difficulties, induced her to drive out with them to Pendeen to hear Mr. Aitken preach on Ascension Day, 1854. She was deeply moved by his sermon, and afterwards yielded to his and Mrs. Aitken's kind persuasions to stay with them till the following day for further counsel and prayer. Many will remember her own vivid account of this memorable visit: how Mr. Aitken's fervid eloquence in prayer and argument, his intensely strong faith and force of character, prevailed over her own hesitancy, and brought home to her in a way she had never before realized the fact of a personal, individual Saviour. How much this "appropriation to herself of the benefits of Redemption" influenced her life thenceforward, may be seen in the following letters. This correspondence with Mr. and Mrs. Aitken was kept up throughout the rest of their lives. Unfortunately the collection of letters preserved is very imperfect, but it is enough to show how firmly she adhered to Mr. Aitken's interpretation of the Gospel, how comforting she found his warm personal interest in her soul's welfare, and his and his wife's constant loving-hearted hospitality and friendship. She used to describe Mr. Aitken as her ideal of a patriarch, and said she felt him a rock to cling to and rest on among all waves of religious trial or depression. But though never deviating from her own strong convictions of the truth, based on his teaching, she was large-hearted enough to appreciate and to help in any earnest work for God from whatever school of thought it proceeded. Of this we have touching proof in the many grateful tributes paid to her memory, quoted later on.

## CHAPTER II.

*Letters to and from Rev. and Mrs. Aitken.*

(1854-82.)

First visit to Pendeen—Conversion—Anxiety for spiritual growth—Letter from Mr. Haslam—Birthdays, 1854-55—Rev. G. Fenton's coming to S. Paul's, Penzance, 1856—Extracts about Father's death, 1857-58—Lizzie Marks—Anniversary of first visit to Pendeen—All Saints' Day—Mr. Aitken's birthday—Captain Bedford's death, 1868—Ascension Day, 1868—Death of Mrs. Aitken's grandchild, 1868—Christmas, 1869—Mr. Aitken's birthday, 1870—Mr. Grant's death, 1870—Ascension Day, 1870—Mrs. Aitken's sister's death, 1872—Birthday, 1877—Remembrance of Mr. Aitken's birthday, 1880—Conversion of old servant, 1882.

Parsonage, Pendeen, *2nd June, 1854.*

My dear Miss Bolitho,—I have been very anxious to hear of your spiritual state, and have rather wondered that we have had no communication. Surely you have not rested, but have gone on to realize the pardoning mercy and saving power of your Lord. But yet I tremble for you, knowing the deceitfulness of the human heart and the cunning and power of the enemy. Much as I would like to hear from you, if you prefer opening your mind to Mr. Aitken, his address is—

*Care of* Vyvyan Moyle, Esq.,
Pembroke College,
Oxford.

There a letter will find him till, I think, the middle of next week; and do give him or me, or both of us, the happiness of knowing that you are not of them who draw back unto perdition, but of them who believe to the saving of the soul. This is no time to trifle and delay. Those who love the Lord have need to be all in earnest to be holy themselves and to live so in the power of His Spirit as to become effectual and successful instruments in calling others out of darkness into His marvellous light.

Shall we heartlessly neglect to walk according to the light vouchsafed to us, and to realize the truths we believe in our minds, and yet expect to escape the condemnation of those who knew and did not their Lord's will—barren and unfruitful cumberers of the ground?

Believe me, my dear Miss Bolitho,
Yours very sincerely,
W. D. AITKEN.

The Coombe, *Monday Morning, June, 1854.*

My dear Mrs. Aitken,—I do indeed feel quite ashamed at not having days ago written to you. Oh! do forgive my seeming ingratitude. I have ever felt afraid to express on paper the state of my soul, nor without a severe struggle to speak of its past concerns, but I do trust and believe that He who has begun (I dare not hide my eyes to that fact) will carry on the good work. I desire never to rest satisfied till I can experience that The Truth has made me free; and I hope I am not presumptuous in saying that I am earnestly seeking to enjoy that liberty of soul for which for years I have been longing. I never felt I could praise God as I have since I saw you, nor have I before been as happy in soul. Oh! I have had many peaceful hours; but oh!

I do so dread to say more than I am quite sure I really experience. I have such a fear of deceiving God or man that I cannot tell you all that is in my heart. And now, Mrs. Aitken, let me again thank you and your good husband for all your truly kind interest in, and efforts for, me. I shall never, never forget that solemn night, and trust it may yet be blessed; and oh! may I still ask for an interest in your prayers? But I must not hide from you that I have a trial to bear that I had not looked for. No doubt my remaining at Pendeen unknown to my friends was a little error of judgment, and as such I am very sorry for it; but you were so very kind, and the opportunity for spiritual teaching that I had for so many years desired seemed so plainly opened, that I felt I could not act otherwise than I did, nor do I for one moment regret it, but am most thankful.

My dear father who has been the very kindest and most indulgent of parents, and who has studied our every want and wish beyond what was almost desired, got most painfully agitated and nervous at my not returning. At eighty-eight I must make every allowance for his feelings, as I am sure he would not willingly be unkind; but when I did return, I saw that though he said nothing he was deeply hurt at my leaving him. I was in hopes that in a few days all would settle down, but after waiting a week without mentioning the subject, I spoke to him on Saturday; but he still feels so pained, and I know at present would not sanction my going to Pendeen, so with great, great sorrow, and many, many tears, I must, till the way again is opened, give up the pleasure I had looked forward to of going to Pendeen and again hearing your husband's faithful soul-stirring and never-to-be-forgotten sermons and prayers. Oh! as I may not (as I had desired) drink of the streams of consolation, do pray that I may from the never-changing, ever-flowing Fountain.

Again thanking you for your very great kindness, allow me to remain, with very kind regards to all your party,

Yours sincerely obliged,<br>E. B. B.

Parsonage, Pendeen, *June 13th, 1854.*

My dear Miss Bolitho,—I give God hearty thanks on your behalf for all the good that I hear of you. Take courage! He who hath begun will also carry on His own work, and if while you work with Him you suffer *Him* to carry it on *in His own way*, it cannot fail to be perfected. Live only by the present moment, but live to God, striving continually to realize His presence. Seek *light*, and life, and power, only that you may the better glorify and serve Him; but if you are *dark*, and *dry*, and *powerless*, still bless *for* these, and bless Him *under* these, and they will soon give place to the glad and satisfied confidence of a child who never knew its father to deceive it. And be not grieved that you may not come here: those happy and favoured children whom God leads into solitude and teaches there, are the best taught. You address Him in church as "the strength of your salvation;" oh! let Him be continually the *strength* of your *weak* heart, and your "portion for ever."

I shall communicate to you, from time to time, the progress of the work of God as far as we may know something of it, as I feel assured you long and pray for the coming of His kingdom. Alas! how shall we all be sifted ere that day arrives?

Before the eight days of his stay at Leeds were ended, Mr. Aitken's labours there were crowned with a most encouraging return. On Sunday, Monday, and Tuesday, there were a few penitents, but on Friday night, after the sermon, between thirty and forty persons found peace with God,—among them were two clergymen, one of whom had no sooner received the remission of sins himself, than he, unaided by any human help, led six or seven other souls successfully to the same glorious sin-pardoning Saviour he himself had found. By my letters to-night another clergyman in great distress had been to Mr. Aitken, enquiring the way of salvation, and not likely to rest till he had found it. Thus there are six converted Catholic clergymen able to carry on conversion or penitent work now in Leeds, and two more probably by this time added to their number. . . . . . I expect Mr. Aitken home to-night from Cuddesden, the Bishop of Oxford's seat. I hope when you are in perplexity you will write to him, and have from him strengthening and encouraging counsel.

With kindest love to you, my dearest Miss Bolitho,
  Yours very affectionately,
    WILHELMINA D. AITKEN.

Here we insert an extract from a letter written about this time, in reply to one from Mrs. Aitken describing Emily Bolitho's spiritual difficulties, evidently with a hope of helping her.

### *From Rev. W. Haslam to Mrs. Aitken.*

. . . . . We heard of Miss Bolitho some weeks since. What can she be waiting for? Many church people who laugh at us for being "Methodists," when they are under convictions prove themselves Methodists in reality! *They will not believe till they feel,*—just as if salvation depended on their *feeling it ! !* It depends on what Christ *has* done and suffered for them. He will not die again—*He has died!* Let her take hold by Faith: what would she do if she felt all that she desires to feel? Let her *do that,* and do it *as if she did feel,* and she will *feel!* Feeling is a *flower;* Faith is the root and plant. Her plant will not flourish, because, like many, I suppose, she plants it with the flowering end downwards;—a very common practice. Simply get her to praise God "with the best member that she has,"— " O Lord, open my mouth, and my lips shall praise Thee,"—and so begin forthwith, "Glory be to God, He died for me!" If she is in earnest she will soon realize the *words.* . . . . . Too many will not give God any praise because they cannot give Him what they would; but He lovingly bids us come just *as we are,* and to bring what we have, and offer that WILLINGLY, and He will accept the *offering and bless and multiply it.* He is sure to do so. . . . . .

---

The Coombe, *Saturday Morning, 1854.*

My dear Mrs. Aitken,—As I know from experience how very refreshing grapes are for the throat when it is at fault, it has struck me that they might be useful for your good husband, who I trust may not suffer from the exertion of to-morrow; and I am sure you will not deprive me of the great pleasure it will give me to think that perhaps the accompanying fruit may give him some little refreshment. Oh! how I should like to be at Pendeen church to-morrow, but I fear I must not attempt to leave home, as my dear father likes me with him on a Sunday. I must again thank you for all your kind interest in me; my visits to Pendeen are quite seasons of refreshment. If I should ever be permitted to come again, I shall hope again to hear from Mr. A—— what he said to me on Tuesday about the two covenants; I cannot quite remember it, and I want to so much. I do feel so thankful to know that you pray for me. Oh! how much do I want to know and praise, and love.

With much love to your party, allow me to remain,

Yours truly obliged,

E. B. B.

Parsonage, Pendeen, *August 1st, 1854.*

My dear Miss Bolitho,—Do let us hear from you, how you are getting on. I long to hear of self-conquest,—of victory over nature, over nerves, over everything that hinders your holy joy and perfect liberty in Him. Forget yourself in pouring out your soul for others; how many you ought to be yearning over so as never to have a moment to spend two thoughts on yourself! Glorify Him, whatever you do. Our love, and prayers, and sympathies, are with you.

In Christ Jesus, your devoted servant,

W. D. AITKEN.

The Coombe, *September 23rd, 1854.*

My dear Mrs. Aitken,—You will not, I hope, think it an intrusion sending you the accompanying grapes, but I think they may be useful to your good husband, who I trust by the week's rest may have gained strength for to-morrow's duties. I was much better both in mind and body for my visit to Pendeen; your kind encouraging *decided* conversation always raises the tone of the former, and your fine air has a wonderful effect on the latter; but my nervous fears still make me think that I am an intruder on your time and patience.

Mrs. G—— has been so frequently the subject of my thoughts; I do hope she has found "peace in believing;" I shall envy her if she has. I do try to bless and praise God for what I have; but oh! I do so want to know and love more. If nothing prevents, I shall try to come to your church to-morrow; I am looking forward with much pleasure to the prospect.

With very kind regards to you all, allow me to remain, dear Mrs. Aitken,

Yours very affectionately,<br>
E. B. BOLITHO.

The Coombe, *October 9th, 1854.*

My dear Mrs. Aitken,—I am longing to see you, and to hear some kind words from you. That dreadful sense of depression has so tried me the last few days, and I cannot look off self though I want to, yet I feel so unequal to the struggle. I believe it may be caused by my not being well, and I suppose it must end in my consenting to get change of air and scene.

Am I troubling you very much if I ask you to send me a little note to-morrow, which I may receive on Wednesday morning,—it being my birthday? I shall feel very thankful to know that you will remember me on that day. I think you will be amused when I tell you, that last evening when I said to Miss Gladstone that I was feeling "weak and depressed in mind and body," her reply was, "You want a visit to Pendeen to set you up again!"

I feel I ought not to break in on your valuable time, or I should try to manage a call this week. Excuse my writing to you again, and please not to think it an intrusion.

I remain, with kind regards to you all,

Your affectionate<br>
E. B. BOLITHO.

Parsonage, Pendeen, *October 10th, 1854.*

My dear Miss Bolitho,—You know very well we shall be glad to see you at Pendeen, and will heartily welcome you whenever you can come; and now you will believe a wretch like me in saying this! and you will (if permitted) come out to Pendeen as soon as you can, with perfect confidence in our sincerity and truth!! And will you yet doubt the love of Him who is *Love* itself? of Him Who is *the Truth*, and Who so graciously says, "I have loved thee with an everlasting love, therefore with loving-kindness have I drawn thee?" There is a depth of self-love, and a wantonness of ingratitude (in sporting thus with unbelief in the very face of God revealed to you in Jesus Christ, pouring out such declarations to you) which I am sure, my dear Miss Bolitho, you do not see, or you would not suffer yourself in. The question is not of *your goodness to God*, but of God's goodness to you; not of *your merits*, but of *His grace*. Has He loved, and does He love you? Thank, bless, and praise Him for a love so generous. Do you not consciously love Him in return? Adore him all the more that He still loves one so unloving! But let no false humility hinder His work in you; remember that any measure of love wrought in you in return is wrought by His Spirit, and of His own make haste and render unto Him.

May every returning 11th October find you, my dearest Miss Bolitho, more and more swallowed up in loving, serving, and glorifying your God! "Sorrowful, yet always rejoicing," let that be your motto; lift up to Him the weeping eye and heavy heart of her who can say, "Thou knowest all things, Thou knowest that *I would* love Thee," and thou shalt rejoice in this confidence evermore. . . . . .

With much love from all of us till we meet,
Yours most affectionately in Christ,
WILHELMINA D. AITKEN.

*9th October, 1855.*

My dear Mrs. Aitken,—Oh! what a trouble you took on yourself when you first invited me to Pendeen. Well! I can't help it; out of the abundance of the heart the pen moves as well as the tongue speaks; the former I want you to move in my service, as I very much wish a long note from you on Thursday morning, as that is my birthday. I heard from you on the 11th of October, 1854, and that note was a great comfort to me. I was in a sad depressed state then; thank God those seasons of trial are not as frequent as they used to be, nor is the cloud always as heavy as it once was. When the train passed our house this morning I was reading the Litany with my father. I did not forget your dear husband, when praying for those who travel by land or water, and I do trust that not only will he be preserved from all outward danger, but that the Lord may prosper his way, and make him the means of glorifying Him by bringing souls to Him. I shall often think of him, and also of you, and endeavour to remember you where I am sure you most wish to be remembered.

We got home very safely, and at the exact time that my father wanted me; I wish I could feel quite easy about the going so far on a Sunday. My cousin and I had not a happy talk last night; I feel my mind much too weak and too unsettled to bear it with profit. Please I was quite angry at your thinking I should not care to come to Pendeen if Mr. Aitken was away. Oh! it is well for you that my way is not made too easy for coming to you, or what a *perpetual blister* you would have! But I will not trouble you with more to-day. With much love, and hoping for a very long note on Thursday, I remain,

Your affectionate<br>E. B. B.

*9th October, 1855.*

My dear Mr. Aitken,—I wished to have gone to the train this morning though I was not sure at what time you would come, but I was prevented doing so,—indeed my life is subject to so many interruptions; I hope sometimes there may be a mission of service even in that; but as I have only a few minutes just now, I must hasten to ask you once more if you will be so very kind as to write me a birthday letter. I shall greatly value it, if it be ever so short. My birthday is on Friday, so if you will write me a note by your next post I shall get it. I hope nothing may prevent my going to Pendeen for the service on Friday evening; I mean to give my sisters Mrs. G——, Mrs. W. B——, and Miss M——, a birthday treat, and bring them. I am to have a large afternoon tea-party before I go, so we shall (D.V.) come direct to church. I hope God will give you some word for us all. I thought much of you yesterday. I have an interesting account to tell you of a girl to whom your Whit-Sunday sermon at St. Paul's was blessed. I hope Mrs. M—— is pretty well, and that you have good accounts from the off ones. Much love.

Your affectionate
E. B. B.


My dear Mrs. Aitken,—I did not mean to trouble you again so soon with a grunting note; but I can't resist the temptation, hoping by this means to get, ere very long, one of your bright fresh notes which always do me good. You see I am selfish to the "back-bone." I thought of you all so often on Sunday; I was not out for the day, but I hope I was not *alone*. I have finished No. 5, and thank your dear husband for it; I often threw it down, and said, "No, not another word will I read," but the next moment was at it more than ever; then the sad depression occasioned by reading but not realizing, and I must own there were some bright gleams when I could praise and bless, and many moments of prayer. Oh! don't you love the collect for this week? (21st Sunday after Trinity), it is always on my lips; oh! to serve God with "a quiet mind;" do pray that I may realize the first three blessings, and then that will follow. I send you a part of a note I had from M. T——, as I think you will like to know what she says about E. H——. The J. M—— of whom she speaks is now staying with us; she is decidedly a seeking soul, but does not realize all that *she might*. Fancy *my* saying that! but I do think others may, and ought not to rest short of realizing what I do not. Oh! how often do I long, aye, and resolve, to seek till I find, but I feel the exercise is quite too much for mind and body; I hope sloth is not at the bottom of this, but when I make the attempts I feel such exhaustion of body and such absence of wanderings of mind; but here I am as usual at self and my feelings. Oh! shall I *ever* be lost, or rather swallowed up, in Another!

How happy and thankful Mr. Aitken must be to see Mr. N——! Another soul given for his hire. What do you mean by being three-fourths an invalid? I really do hope there is not much amiss. Will it excite Miss H—— your telling her how thankful I feel that she remembers my dear father in her prayers? Oh! at evening time I do trust there will be light. With much love,

Your much obliged and affectionate
E. B. B.

The Coombe, *Monday Morning, 1856.*

My dear Mrs. Aitken,—I trust your dear invalid does not lose ground, and that you are able to enjoy his society; with such a large party in the house I feel as if my coming for a few hours even would be almost an intrusion, but still, if I can leave home, I shall endeavour to see you ere the week closes. I wish I could praise and thank God more for sending good Mr. Fenton[1] here; I feel sure he will be a blessing, and is already in full work amongst the poor. I had the pleasure of hearing him preach last evening. Eloquent he will never be, but, thank God, I have quite outlived looking for that only, and every word seemed full of unction, and to me it came with much love and power. He has himself asked me to come with him to-day, and receive the communion with a dying man in whom for many months I have been deeply interested, and who said to me on Saturday, "I am too weak to speak to you, but I am not too weak to praise God;" and the holy, happy smile that lit up his face went straight to my heart. Mr. Fenton has been so kind as to say he will come here this evening and meet our school-mistress. I thank God she does not go back, though not as decidedly forward as you could desire. A—— gave her half-an-hour on Friday, and asked her to spend that night in prayer, which she did, and almost all of Saturday she was in the school-room alone. I gave her a little time since, "Fletcher's address to those who say, 'What can I do to be saved?'" She told me yesterday she felt that book was doing her good, and that she was resolved never to go back; she is most anxious to come to Pendeen again. I tell her I will not prevent her doing so, but that I fear it is too much like trusting to man's help alone. My good kind friend Miss M—— is in great trouble; her sister is most alarmingly ill, continued bleeding from the lungs; she has had two previous attacks, but not as severe as this; but, poor thing, she has

---

[1] Rev. George Fenton, for many years in charge of S. Paul's. He married her niece, Minnie Gregory.

been most strong in resisting grace; do pray for her. The carriage is waiting for me, so as usual, in haste, good-bye. With very much love to you all,

Your very affectionate

E. B. B.

The Coombe, *Tuesday Morning*.

My dear Mrs. Aitken,—For many days my time and thoughts have been much engaged, but I have not forgotten you, and hope ere this you are quite yourself again. I was in-doors several days last week (from a cold again), and such loss of voice, indeed now I am not fit for much, though out again and better, and am looking forward to the services on Wednesday and Thursday; we had such a profitable sermon at Leskinnick yesterday. But M. T—— and I have been deeply interested in a case in this house. Please to tell Mr. Aitken, but mention no name to anyone else, as at present she is very particular on that point, and is anxious that her life shall prove that she is indeed the Lord's. Yes, and the work has indeed been His, and to Him be all the glory. Man in this case proposed, but God has indeed disposed to the frustrating of man's opinions and advice. It is a long story, but when we meet I shall be so happy to tell you all, and your dear husband too (the very one she was warned against) has been one of the instruments used; but oh! to see her so humbled, so teachable, it is such a blessed change. M. T—— has been a great help, and Mr. Fenton so indefatigable.

Dear F—— (you know I do feel her so very dear) had to leave us last night, and her present is a most trying position; but He who has done such great things for her can strengthen her, and oh! may His angel keep her in all her ways. I feel I must go and see her this morning, and to hear if she can rejoice in the

Psalm for the day, "And He hath put a new song in my mouth;" but I must not say more, as papa is waiting for me. I hope dear Mr. Aitken will see him, yes, and her too, during his visit; and now with very much love to you all,

    I remain, dear Mrs. Aitken,
       Your very affectionate
          E. B. B.

      The Coombe, *December 12th, 1857.*

My dear Mrs. Aitken,—How can I thank you for that much valued gift? I did so enjoy it when I opened the parcel; but as Mr. Fenton was in the room I could not be very demonstrative, and in a few minutes the dear original came, and *then* I quite forgot *the picture*. I do feel so much obliged to you, and oh! if your dear husband's picture is so precious to those who love him, oh! what will it be when we see *Him* Whom not having seen we love (yes, even I *do* love Him, but oh! so coldly. Oh! that my entire heart was His, and never more mine). Since Mr. Aitken left I have had a few very hopeful moments with my dear father; oh! I do trust that we shall yet rejoice together. . . . . .

It is time to send this, so with my best love, and very many thanks,
    I remain, your very affectionate
         E. B. BOLITHO.

        The Coombe, *1857.*

My dear Mrs. Aitken,—These bright mornings are most tempting, and make me long for a drive to Pendeen (not that I ever need any extra inducement to bend my steps in that direction), but my poor dear sister and her daughters I send for a country drive each morning, and indeed I cannot leave papa, he has not been quite well the last few days—nothing to make me really uneasy I hope, but still I must feel anxious at any little indisposition at his advanced age. . . . . . I know I am not half enough in earnest on the subject of his soul, but nothing seems to make me realize the unseen things, I have far too much to do with the seen. . . . . .

Here I was interrupted to go to papa; I had some conversation with him that did interest me, and sometimes I am led to hope that he does realize more than we think. He told me this morning that he did believe Jesus Christ died for him, and afterwards most earnestly said, "I know that my Redeemer liveth!" I feel he is too weak to exercise the mind, nor can he keep it fixed on any subject, but I do desire to bless God for any gleams of hope. Oh! this morning how I did long for your dear husband. To Mr. Trembath I shall ever feel most thankful for his help: he is so kind, and so good and faithful to souls. . . . .

Your very affectionate<br>E. B. BOLITHO.

*January 1st, 1858.*

My very dear Mrs. Aitken,—From the Smiths yesterday you heard of our own beloved father; he still goes on without any great change. . . . . . It is indeed a waiting time, . . . . . the restlessness is most distressing; we find a verse of a hymn or text quiets him. Trembath was here this morning and he prayed with him, and he seemed to enter into it. My mind and body are so worn out that I feel so very indifferent; I trust this waiting time may be good. I, too, had my "watch-night," and I trust it was a very profitable season; it was so perfectly quiet in the sick chamber, as dear papa had a quiet night. I know you pray for me; I do so deeply feel the kindness of my dear friends.

Ask your dear husband to send me a text as a motto for the year. I well remember his last; this promises to be an eventful one to me, but as yet I have been kept from all anxious thoughts as to the future.

With love and best wishes,

I remain, your loving

E. B. BOLITHO.

The Coombe, *Tuesday, 4 p.m., January, 1858.*

My dear Mrs. Aitken,—Our precious sufferer still goes on; I dare not think he can last many days, though I do not for one moment realize what it will be when I see him really gone, so actively am I now employed with him. . . . . . Cease not to pray for him and for me, indeed for us all. Oh! may we all get blessing from this sad, sad trial; I never felt so withdrawn from the world, and too much shrink from the every day duties; I feel so afraid of myself. Oh! may the Lord be a stronghold! I am sure He will be; I can, I do trust Him. . . . . .

*Friday, 3 p.m.*

. . . . . Our dear one still lingers. We have been watching for his last breath all the morning; he is sensible, and tried to follow me when I said some verses. . . . . . Please pray for me, I do so want it; and do pray that my will and spirit may be brought down; it does rise terribly sometimes, I cannot yet realize the solemn scenes through which we are passing.[1] . . . .

Your very affectionate

E. B. B.

\* \* \* \* \* \* \* \* \* \* \* \*

The Coombe, *Friday Night (about 1860).*

My very dear Mrs. Aitken,—I thank you much for your kind letter, but oh! I am so pained that you thought I had forgotten

---

[1] Mr. Bolitho's death occurred January 11th, but we have no letters referring to it.

you, and well you might think it, never having heard from me; but more than a month since I enclosed a letter for you to Mr. Aitken, not knowing your address, and that dear naughty man could not have forwarded it; and to be honest, I must allow I thought you very slow in answering it. I do think very much about you, and oh! may rich blessings rest on dear Willie's[1] labours. I do remember you where I am sure you most wish to be remembered. I have an idea in my head of going to Pendeen to-morrow; I have only once been able to get there since you left; but I had one day's holiday, and that was indeed a happy day. Mr. Haslam was so very unwell that he was spending a few days with me for a little change, and one morning I took Mrs. Haslam and himself to Pendeen. We intended to dig your dear husband out of his den, and take him off somewhere with us, but he would not move, so we sat on the grass and ate our dinner there; and oh! dear Mr. Aitken was so charming and nice. I think he talked to us there for nearly three hours, and then we went into the church, and there he prayed *as* he prays; and then we went up to the top of the hill and enjoyed that, and then back to the Parsonage to tea, and into Penzance in time for church. Oh! I shall not soon forget that happy day; I wish you could have enjoyed it with us. I could only think of millenium times. This week I have been at Plymouth with my poor dear afflicted sister, Mrs. G——. . . . . .

*Nov. 6th, 1861.*

My dear Mrs. Aitken,—Daily have I thought of you and much wished to have seen you. . . . . I heard from Mr. Savage[2] that you have had favourable reports of your dear husband; I am so

---

[1] Mr. Aitken's son, Rev. W. Hay M. H. Aitken, the Mission Preacher.
[2] Rev. George Savage, Curate of S. Paul's, afterwards married Miss Mary Aitken.

thankful to get this news. How often did I think the day they left Penzance what a lovely train that must be! Two such dear holy men of God; I do think there must have been a delightful feeling in the atmosphere, and I longed to partake of it; how you must miss them ! . . . . .

I have a nervous feeling about giving up the little "gatherings" that we have each week, though there is not as much apparent fruit as we could desire; still I do desire to plough and sow in hope, and do feel thankful to be allowed in the very humblest way to be enabled to work for God. On Sunday week, when some people got hold of the hope that your dear brother might be at my school-room, I had more than 50 women; and last Sunday 36. God helps me, but I feel more and more frightened. Last night I again assembled the men; I gave it up in the summer, as they were working in their gardens late. Eight men and four boys came. Will you pray for me? I do feel so weak and so devoid of love. Oh! such terrible depression the last few days. But it is time to get ready for church; I feel very inclined to sit at home by the fire, for I am not feeling strong. Will you give my love to Mr. Aitken, and to Mr. Grant too, when you write. I would write to the former, but really am so dull and stupid I would not inflict a letter on him; but I shall be so glad to see him back again. Kindest love to M. and E.

Your very affectionate<br>E. B. B.

The Coombe, *Tuesday Night, 1862.*

My dearest Mrs. Aitken,— . . . . . I don't realize the value of souls, nor the reality of eternity. I do pray to be made more sensible of the unseen and to be less taken up with the seen, and

I think I do far less mind earthly things, but I know **nothing of heavenly** things. . . . . .

Oh! how I did enjoy a sight of dear Miss Powell this afternoon; her sympathy is so sweet. Yesterday I spent a few minutes with dear Lizzie Marks; she is decidedly losing **ground,** but is in such a satisfactory state of mind, so quietly **waiting her** Heavenly Father's will, and seems to have no wish but to be where He will have her be. She said to me this **morning,** "Mother has been reading to me about Peter's wife's mother,— as soon as the fever left her she rose and ministered; **and I** looked up and said, 'Lord, what wilt Thou have me do?' In a moment the answer came, 'Preach and teach, and I will **put My** law into thy lips.'" The dear girl said all this so simply, and the dear old woman—she is so happy; but she has not **dear** Lizzie's mind nor education; but her simple faith and **constant** praise I quite envy. She said to me, "Christ is with me **when I** go out, and when I come in; I give myself to Him when I lie down, and He is with me when I awake; I have all in Him, **and** He is my all, and the world is nothing to me;" it is indeed a happy household. I am sure if Joseph was sent into Egypt **to** save life, they went to Penzance to save their souls. Dear **M.** T—— is still very unwell, quite laid aside, and so cut off from all outward help. Oh! dear Mrs. Aitken, what ought I to be **with** all my privileges. Mr. Fenton preached so strikingly a week **ago** on the character of the Nazarite; oh! to be one. Much love.

Your very loving<br>E. B. B.

The Coombe, *May 25th, 1863.*

My very dear Mrs. Aitken,—This day nine years I first visited Pendeen; I had arranged a little plan in my own mind that I might spend an hour or two with you to-day, but I am so very, very disappointed, the coachman is obliged to go to St. Ives, so I must give up the expected pleasure, though it has not been without tears, for I am very foolish, and don't get over as I ought the being dependent on others for a carriage. I feel strongly tempted to hire a carriage, but I think, with so many urgent calls for one's money, for my own selfish gratification it would not be right; but I feel I must just write you a little note. I do indeed thank God that He directed my steps to you on that day, and I do feel truly grateful to you and dear Mr. Aitken for all your kindness to me. I am very ashamed of my own low state of Christianity. I have received much good seed, but the heart has not been honest, and the thorns, the weeds, and the other things have too often all but entirely choked it. I can bless God for the little spark of grace that is not extinguished. Oh! may He by His Holy Spirit's power yet fan it into a flame. Nothing but His own power can do this; but oh! my heart seems so encased in hardness and unbelief, everything that is un-Christlike—but I shall be late for the post, so must close this. I look forward to seeing and hearing your dear husband on Wednesday evening. I know it is useless to ask him to come to see me. . . . . .

Love for all your dear party.

Your affectionate and deeply obliged
E. B. B.

The Coombe, *1864.*

My dear Mr. Aitken,—Thank you very much for your very kind letter, and for your wishing to hear from me again. I do thank God for having so abundantly blessed your labours. The Gospel for the week has been much in my mind; God grant that these late converts may have received the seed into good ground, and that it may take deep root downwards, and bear much fruit upwards. Every time I read that parable it seems more plain that it is from ourselves that the seed does not take root and bear fruit. Oh, those cares that do so choke! But lately I have been kept so free from any anxious thought; fear of man, and not liking to be singular are my present temptations. Dear M. T—— and I are still quietly here together, thankfully receiving our present blessing with very little thought as to future arrangements. . . . . .

We are very glad to have Mr. Fenton back; he looks ill, but is as active and full of love for his Master and His cause as ever. He is such a living epistle, that he must be blessed to souls. . . .

The Coombe, *All Saints' Day, 1865.*

My dear Mr. Aitken,—I should like to be at Pendeen and hear you talk a little about the saints above, and urge us on to be saints below. Well the church shows her idea of saints in the Gospel for the day, and the King of Saints Who spake those words knew who were the truly blessed, but oh! it is so easy to talk about it, but I want to *be it*, and yet I know I don't like, and I shrink from, the needed discipline. These quiet thoughts and words are always rising, and then the terrible depression and doubting that follow! But, bless God, the precious departed ones have overcome, and His grace is still the same, and oh! may He enable me the more to look at "The Author and Finisher of our faith," and thus to lay aside the weights that so draw and fix me down to earth. How very perfect is the chain of all the service to-day; the 1st Psalm, too, seemed so earnest and full of teaching,—it is those who make His law their study and delight that shall be like fruitful trees by the water-side. We had a very blessed Communion this morning; God greatly helps our dear pastor,—he is better far than I expected to see him; I don't think I ever valued him as much; his sermon on Sunday evening, from the words, "Almost thou persuadest me to be a Christian," was very powerful. One lady asked me to-day if I had not thought him a little hard; I told her "No," for the last three months we have had too easy teaching. Dear Minnie has been a little better to-day, and has been out for a short time in a close carriage. I have only seen her once; her voice is stronger, and she is cheerful, but the state of the pulse must tell on her strength. Mr. Fenton speaks of them as 145 and 150; her cough is troublesome indeed; disease is taking its course, and ere another "All Saints' Day" she will, I doubt not, have joined the church above. I went to the service at St. Mary's yesterday, on the opening of the new bells. The Church Service was very nicely performed, and there were many solemn remarks in the sermon. How often do I think of your last sermon at St. Paul's, on the words "Make the men sit down." Oh! it is so true they will not consider; they are hurried on in the stream; and oh! where will it end? How is it I feel so little real love for souls?

For the last year I have been constantly visiting a Mrs. B——, a little Irish widow in consumption. I went to see her yesterday, and found that she was dead; at the last it was so very sudden. She told me a few days since that she was happy that Jesus was with her, and that she felt communion with Him, adding, "It would indeed be sad to be as I am now without Him;" but yet, Mr. Aitken, I never felt happy about her, and there was so little power in what she said; and I felt it always so difficult to speak or pray with her. We were to have had the Holy Communion with her at three to-morrow, but we shall meet no more on earth.

I had such an interesting little talk with Mr. Shortland, the Roman Catholic priest, this morning; I always yearn over that dear little man. This time twenty years he was so kind and full of sympathy to me when I was in deep sorrow;—but the length of my letter shocks me.

I hope you are all pretty well? Much love for you all

Your affectionate and obliged

E. B. B.

*January 21st, 1866.*[1]

My dear Mr. Aitken—I had in my own mind arranged some weeks since that I would, if possible, spend a little time at Pendeen on the 21st, but since last Saturday I have been quite confined to the house with a bad cough, and Mr. Dodge says whilst the frost lasts I must not venture out, so I must just send you a message of love and my very best wishes and prayers that God's blessing may abundantly rest on you; that He may fill you with Himself, and use you for His glory. I often long to see more of you, but I know, like the disciples we have read of to-day, I like to make earthly tabernacles; but if it be to see "No man but Jesus only," and He reveals more of Himself and gives me the ear to hear Him, I dare not grieve, as I now too often do, over the remembrance of past happy days. . . . . .

Mr. R—— spent Monday evening with me; it was a most edifying visit; but do urge on him not doing too much, and also on his visiting a little more the (in the world's eyes) respectable part of his congregation. It is six years on Monday since dear J. B—— found peace with God; I trust he is now for ever with Him. On Monday, too, my brother will be fifty-eight; do pray for him. Please accept the little substantial proof of my sweet feelings, and with much love for you all,

I remain, your very affectionate and obliged,

E. B. B.

[1] Mr. Aitken's Birthday.

The Coombe, *Tuesday Morning, 1866.*

My very dear Mrs. Aitken,—I went to the railway station last Friday hoping for a peep of you, but was disappointed. I had not been home for many hours, so did not get your letter; on my return I received it; thank you for it. I often think what a nice happy party you must be at Torquay, and almost long for a peep at you. I hope as the weather changes Eda[1] may get rid of her cough. I could wish for a better report of your precious brother, but this "coming apart to rest awhile" is, we are sure, for good among the "all things" that He Who is Love is "working out" for his benefit.

Willie and Robert walked back with me from the station on Friday; the former kindly gave me a little help with a sick man in our village, and his prayer was a great comfort to me, for I was dreadfully down last week. I often thought of all Mr. Grant[2] had said, but got a great lift by the last verse of 1 John, i.—"If we confess our sins He is faithful and just to forgive us our sins."

I am hoping to see and hear dear Mr. Aitken at York House to-morrow; I was not there last time, my throat kept me a prisoner for a week. God does not leave us without a blessing here. A man found peace at Mr. Fenton's house on Sunday night; a sick boy and a consumptive girl last week; and I hope there may be many more, but these are all I know just lately. M. A. M—— and H. H—— are deeply interested in a girl; she does not like me, and though I have called four times have only seen her twice. She has a very proud, unsubdued spirit, but I trust that she may be led to Jesus. I have a very interesting young woman near me, a cousin of Lizzie Marks; in the house where L—— died, she was converted last November, but about a fortnight since God gave her such a *sight* of herself. Oh! for days she had no rest night nor day,—every sin came so before

---

1 Miss E. Aitken married Dr. H. Nankivell.  2 Mr. H. W. Grant, Mrs. Aitken's brother.

her. She could praise God all the time, and never once doubted that she was His child; sometimes she was *filled* with the Holy Ghost, and would praise and sing for hours. I need not tell you that the enemy of her soul did not fail to take advantage of the weakness of her body, and his temptations were fearful. Often he would persuade her she had never been ill, and more than once she got out of bed and fell on the floor, but at last she said, "Well, never mind if I am not ill, and if I need not have remained in bed, it has brought me to Jesus, and He has saved my soul here." A few days since, when I was with her, she put her hands up to her ears, dragged out her ear-rings, and dashed them on the floor, and said to her sister, "Take all the flounces off my dress, put away my hat and feathers, and have the straw hat made into a bonnet that I may go to God's house." I think her health is recovering, and I do trust that the work in her soul is deep.

Did I tell you of Mrs. S——'s conversion? Her husband is a clergyman, and succeeded Mr. G—— at the Grammar School. At our little Saturday evening prayer-meeting we have been praying for her for months; she was such a regular "Daughter of Jerusalem." She is now ill, and the Sunday Mr. Aitken was at Hayle, Mr. S——, not being well, wished Mr. Fenton to take his place at the jail; Mr. Fenton could not, and called to say so. Mrs. S—— heard he was in the house, and said she wished to see him, and he called on her again the next day, telling her to praise God for what He had done. After he was gone, she did so, and oh, such light and peace filled her soul! She goes on so nicely; I often see her, and she is so bold in telling every one what God has done for her. Poor Mr. H. P—— is very, very ill,—hopelessly so; he knows his *bodily* danger, but I can say no more. He will not see a creature but his wife; I hear she prays with him, and I know many are doing so for him. . . . . . Such a nice work going on at Hayle amongst the sailors, thank God. . . . .

Pendeen, *23rd January, 1867.*

My dearest Emily,—Many and hearty thanks for your most kind wishes, but oh! this '67 makes one very thoughtful. Within three years of the appointed time of man, and yet how little rendering again has there been for all His benefits! Oh, pray! and pray earnestly that the few remaining days may be spent to some abiding purpose. I have no excuse for not being a true saint, for I am unmistakeably dead to everything else but the one desire to be conformed to the will of God, and yet what hinders I know not. It is truly terrible to be so far behind the Pattern which is so clearly placed before us; to be sons of God and yet to have so little of His power; to be sons of God and yet to be so unlike Him; to have such high promises given to us and yet to fall so far short of their realization! Lord, help us! and take us not out of this weary world until it is otherwise with us than it is now. Oh, Thou Hearer and Answerer of prayer, be a Hearer and Answerer of prayer to me! Blessed be God for His undeserved mercies! but oh, how I long to have His favour, to have His confidence, to have that intimacy of fellowship which the soul craves, and nothing less than which will satisfy it!

May God bless you, and be your Helper and your Joy always.

Ever yours most affectionately,<br>R. AITKEN.

The Coombe, *March 3rd, 1868.*

My dear Mrs. Aitken,—I hope you got home safely; I was so glad to have a little visit from you, and wish you would come oftener. As I know you take a kind interest in Captain Bedford's[1] illness I just send you a line to tell you that his earthly warfare is over. For some days it was evident his end was not far off, indeed all yesterday the symptoms were such as to tell us his hours would be few; the restlessness was most distressing till about twelve to-day, and at one o'clock his spirit had passed from earth; he was rarely conscious, but often said, "Going,—going home." When F—— put his Bible into his hand he said, "Oh, the Book!" and sometimes a verse would give a few moments' quiet. He has entered into rest. I think I told you that he said "I have been there, and have seen dear J—— and dear F——; don't weep for them, they are there; I am going to them and you must come too." Oh, if in God's hands his death be made a means of bringing life to some dead soul! oh, what cause for joy would his removal be! Do pray for it. . . . .

Pendeen, *Ascension Day, 1868.*

My dearest Emily,—Our re-creating after the image of Christ in righteousness and true holiness is slow work, because there are so many hindrances, and our will shrinks from conformity to the will of God, hence the formation of Christ in us by the Spirit is a distressingly protracted work indeed, and often-times causing both perplexity and depression. I thank God that there is no inclination to bring down God's standard to your level. You believe that Christ is our second Adam, and has life in Himself as such to impart to us, and that is His own life. Oh! what words—"The glory which Thou gavest Me have I given them;" "As we have borne the image of the earthy, we must also bear the image of the heavenly;" "As Christ is, so are we in this present world;" "As is the heavenly, such are they that are

---

[1] Capt. Tench Bedford, brother to Capt. D. B. Bedford who married her sister Fanny.

heavenly; and "We are to be changed from glory to glory, even as by the Spirit of the Lord." Such is the new creation after the image of Him that created us; in other words, we are in as full a sense to receive the nature of the second Adam as we inherited the nature of the first Adam. The union of the human with the Divine was God's original purpose in creating man. He has never abandoned it, hence it is one glorious destiny. What a different Church and world would they be if we were all striving for the prize of our high calling, instead of finding fault with, differing from, and quarrelling with each other. Oh! how paltry and contemptible are our party prejudices and party strifes in the light of eternity, and with so glorious a prize held out unto us. I thank you for your refreshing letter, for you are evidently getting out of the serious fault of despising the day of small things; it is good to be thankful, and how much have we to be thankful for!

As to your question, the love of Mary Magdalen to our Lord was pure and holy; but most certainly she did not realize the truth in fulness, that He was God as well as man, else she would never have believed that the grave could detain Him, and would not have brought spices to embalm His body; her "Rabboni" had more of pure nature in it than was consistent with her altered relationship to her risen Lord. St. John never again attempted to recline upon His bosom. After His Ascension He intimated that she might then by faith wash His feet again, and wipe them with her hair, but she was no longer to approach Him "as the Mount which might be touched." Immediately afterwards He allowed the other women to hold him by the feet and to worship Him. Mary was strong enough to be taught; and doubtless understood her lesson. . . . . . . . .

. . . . . . . . . . I have pretty hopeful accounts of dearest Eda. . . . . . . .

Ever yours most affectionately,
R. AITKEN.

The Lord bless and keep you, and cause the light of His most loving countenance to shine upon you always. Amen.

The Coombe, *June 9th*.

My very dear Mrs. Aitken,—I heard through Mrs. B—— of the death of your dear little grandson; precious little treasure! how lengthened was his illness! but now, thank God, his warfare *is* accomplished, and he, who never spoke on earth, can now praise his Redeemer; as Leighton says,—" He is but gone to bed an hour or two sooner, whilst we are undressing to follow, and the more we put off of these earthly garments the less we shall have to do when we lie down." Poor dear Alice! but the Lord will strengthen her, and I believe she will feel thankful that her darling is safe with Jesus, and she will not again have the pain of parting from him. Give my kindest love to her, and tell her I didn't forget her and poor dear Mary. He was indeed her little treasure. Our psalm this morning has comforted me very much (45); when we realize our real position we then can enter into verses 10 and 11. I would not intrude a visit on you now, but tell me plainly if you think Alice would think it attention to her attending the dear baby's funeral? If so, I will (D.V.) willingly come,—of course go direct to the church, so as to be no trouble to you.

Yours, with very much love,
E. B. BOLITHO.

The Coombe, *October 30th, 1868.*

Dear Mr. Aitken,—I am going to be very good!! What an assertion! but the case is just this: "All Saints'" Day is one that is very dear to me, and during the nine years dear Mr. Fenton was with us he always encouraged my love for it, or rather, for all it brings to mind. . . . . . I did hope Mr. R——would have had the Celebration of the Holy Communion on Thursday morning, and then several of us wished to come to your service in the evening: but he gave out the Communion for Thursday evening. Now if Emily Bolitho would please herself, she would go to the service and Communion at St. Mary's on Thursday, and come to Pendeen in the evening; but perhaps it would not be kind to Mr. R——, and I think we should strengthen his hands, and the Spirit of the Gospel for All Saints' Day would, I think, tell us not to go away; but yet, dear Mr. Aitken, am I not to have one word about that "part of the host" who "have crossed the flood," and be encouraged by the strength the King of Saints gave them to follow the dear departed ones? Now do tell me what we should do? as several want to come. . . . . . .

The Coombe, *Christmas, 1869.*

. . . . . The clock has just struck twelve, and I must prepare for bed, but not till I have written a line to you, though perhaps I may get to Pendeen before this note, as, if the weather be fine, and carriage and horse disengaged, I should like to spend one hour with you; but if I should be prevented, I write a line to tell you I shall be quite *hurt* and *offended* if you refuse me the pleasure of sending you a Christmas turkey, as I have been allowed to do for some years. I will, all being well, send it with, or rather by, the lads who come for the greens, etc.

...... That hymn of Luther's so expresses my desires: "Make Thee a bed soft, undefiled, within my heart, that it may be a quiet chamber kept for Thee." God helping me I will not forget Willie at Stroud. Mrs. B—— has had a very interesting letter from Miss Y—— about the Mission Work at St. Peter's, Haymarket. Good night. Love for you both. Oh! to have some grasp of His love Who emptied Himself of all but love.

Yours affectionately,

E. B. B.

The Coombe, *January 21st, 1870.*

My dear Mr. Aitken,—Your birthday must not pass without my sending you a few words of loving remembrance to convey my best wishes. You have reached the "three score years and ten," but if our Lord tarry, I trust He may see fit to prolong your life, and to use you still more for His glory, and at last, as a shock of corn fully ripe, He may gather you into His garner, there to meet many whom He gave you grace to help there; when he who soweth and he who reapeth shall rejoice together, and when all the glory and praise shall be unto Him who loved us so. I shall often think of you to-morrow, and thank God that He ever allowed me to know you. I often feel I disappointed you, and still more Him Who I know it is a sin so to doubt. I feel very thankful to know you pray for dear B——, it is the vortex of "other things" that so keeps him and Satan uses to prevent the good seed working. It is nine years to-morrow since dear J. B—— found the Saviour in Whose presence I trust he now is.

The 25th (Conversion of St. Paul) will give you its own subject. Oh, what daily cause have we to praise God for the blessed event we celebrate on that day! Mr. S—— will, I hope, be made very useful; he is a very superior preacher, and seems so to feel all he says. His sermon at St. Paul's last Tuesday was so very, very solemn, on "How shall we escape if we neglect so great salvation?" Often as I have heard that verse made the subject for a text, I don't think I ever saw it so powerfully handled; the law and the Gospel most fully shewn. I felt I could praise God for the great salvation, but oh! I could weep and groan for having so slighted it. But my long letter will have tired you, and you will say there is nothing in it; but please accept much love and gratitude, and with every good wish for you all,

I remain, dear Mr. Aitken,<br>
Yours very truly obliged,<br>
E. B. B.

The Coombe, March 14th, 1870.

My dear Mr. Aitken,—Robert gave me a very indifferent account of you on Saturday, and until the weather quite changes and becomes much milder, I don't fancy you will be much better, as I know when once your delicate bronchial tubes get wrong they do not recover quickly. I very much wish Mrs. Aitken was at home, or that you were nearer your friends. I know you will say it is quite best as it is, and I believe when you are alone you do feel much of God's presence; and I do trust He has been very present of late.

> "Who hath the Father and the Son
> May be left, but not alone."

Reading Joshua always brings your teaching so before me. We had deeply interesting sermons on that subject yesterday;

I do trust they may not have been preached in vain. One lady, a stranger here, was so struck, she says unless she had previously read "High Truths" she should not have understood them. In the evening, the sending for the Ark when the Philistines were getting the advantage over Israel was so striking and terribly true. I got much helped in the morning by the teaching of the Israelites eating the old corn of the land. Oh! Mr. Aitken, the power in the soul and not the head is what I want.

I almost daily expect to hear that dear Mr. Grant has passed away, as from all accounts there seems little hope of his life being prolonged. . . . . .

*March, 1870.*

My dearest Mrs. Aitken,—For days I have wished to write to you, but felt I dare not intrude on your sacred grief; but I feel as if I could no longer forbear sending you a few lines to assure you of my loving sympathy,—constantly are you in my thoughts. I know how your dear warm heart is crushed by this deep sorrow, for you mourn the loss of no ordinary man;[1] but I know after a time you will rise superior even to this separation, knowing it is not for long, and that dear departed one's warfare is accomplished, and he at rest. "A mighty man has fallen!" Oh! may a double portion of his spirit fall on some one, who may God send in mercy to work as faithfully in His church. How thankful you must be that you were allowed to minister to your beloved brother during his last days! I know that at present this will make the fearful blank more felt, but by-and-by it will be so precious to remember. . . .

[1] Mrs. Aitken's brother, Mr. Grant.

The Coombe, *May 25th, 1870.*

My dear Mrs. Aitken,—It is after eleven, and I am so sleepy I can scarcely hold my pen, but I cannot let Ascension Day pass without having some communication with you, and again thanking God for His having directed my way to Pendeen on that, to me, ever memorable Ascension Tide, 1854. I feel ashamed to write that date and to remember so long a time has passed and so little fruit resulted; I know it might have been very different if I had been more faithful in the use of grace received, and drawn more largely from His inexhaustible fulness, but still His goodness and mercy have indeed followed me. I do so want to be delivered from "the other things" that so draw me away and hinder my full "heart and mind" ascending. How I long to have the heart so knit to Him that all else might be forgotten; but I really am too tired to write more. I should so like to see you to-morrow, and to hear some burning message of love from our Ascended Head.

Much love and many thanks for you both, from

Your very affectionate and grateful

E. B. B.

The Coombe, *March 28th, 1871.*

My very dear Mr. Aitken,—M. T—— and I had that moment risen from our knees, where we had been praying for you, when your most interesting letter was put into my hands; thank you very much for it. I feel it was most undeserved kindness. I have daily intended to write to you, but for two reasons have not done so: the first was, I thought you were so fully and so blessedly occupied that I dare scarcely intrude one of my half-hearted, stupid letters; I always think they are very like Pharaoh's asking Jacob "How old art thou?" and

*The Coombe, August 16th, 1872.*

My dear Mrs. Aitken,—I was very much grieved to hear that dear Mr. Aitken had been so unwell, and was very thankful when I went to 15 Alma Terrace, yesterday, to find he was well enough to drive into Penzance, though sorry for the cause of his doing so. I am sure your warm heart must deeply feel the loss of your sister, for though you had rarely the opportunity of meeting, still it was a pleasure to get letters and to feel interested in each other's interests and welfare. One by one your dear ones are reaching home; and thank God the one whose loss you are now called to mourn knew and loved Him Who had loved her, and given Himself for her, and is, I trust, as the shock of corn fully ripe, gathered into the heavenly garner. I know your dear husband would say it implies much to be fully ripe, and truly it does. Our lesson for this evening, Jer. xxiii., has a blessed verse,—" The Lord our Righteousness." I intended this very day to have called on your sister; she has, I trust, recovered from the fatigue of her journey, but I shall defer it for the present, as I know you do not like to see any one when trouble is fresh on you. I shall be very pleased to receive Mr. Aitken on Saturday, if he would like the undisturbed quiet which I will promise him at The Coombe. Much love,

Yours affectionately,

E. B. BOLITHO.

*Falklands, January 21st, 1873.*[1]

My very dear Mr. Aitken,—I must send you just a word or two to give you my best love and every good wish. I do

---

[1] His last birthday; Mr. Aitken died very suddenly on 11th July of this year. Accounts of the event will be found in the next chapter.

bless God for your creation, and trust it may be His will to spare your valuable life to work for Him in leading sinners to Him, and making believers sensible of their high and holy calling to follow Him and strive to become like Him. . . . .

*The Coombe, Festival of S. Philip and S. James, 1873.*

My dear Mrs. Aitken,—Ere this I have intended to write and enquire for your dear husband; but I have the last week had so many interruptions that it has been impossible to do so. I do trust the change and quiet and medical treatment are, by God's blessing, of great service to him, and that he may return with renewed health. You too, are, I hope, well, and enjoying the society of your dearly-loved ones. I know you will long and deeply feel the loss of your long-loved old friend, and miss your constant opportunities of ministering to her, though I am sure you feel thankful that she is "safe home." I hope your sister and Eda are tolerably well, and the wee baby thriving. D—— is a never-ending source of amusement, and I dare say that dear man is "led by a little child." I should like to peep in on you. I am sure it does give dear Mr. Fenton great pleasure to know your dear husband is near him, and they will, I trust, have some holy, blessed, and edifying seasons together. M. T——, too, has been delighted to see you; the weather, too, is so nice,—it has been very warm to-day, and will, I hope, be fine to-morrow, as thirty-five I expect at breakfast. They could not assemble as usual on May-day morning, as they were all too tired after the part they took at the wedding of my niece. . . . .

R——'s three sermons this week were masterly, and so deeply practical and spiritual. Sunday, on "Arise, O Lord, and scatter

Thine enemies;" and in the evening, on the enemy being delivered into Ahab's hand, and he not slaying him. On Tuesday, Christ being Himself the Tabernacle, represented Priest, Mercy-seat, Aaron's Rod, Pot of Manna, etc., etc.

Mr. G――, the clergyman of Godolphin, has died from small-pox; he has several times preached at St. Paul's. I did not like his sermons, but still I dare not say he did not preach there Jesus as the sinner's Saviour; he was, I fancy, liked in his parish; a kind man. He was very much afraid of small-pox, but visited the sick of that disease, and took his death from visiting a sick lad. But I must prepare for bed,—so good night.

Very kind love for you all,

I remain, your very affectionate

E. B. B.

Penmellyn, *October 10th, 1877.*

Dearest Emily,—With all my heart I thank our gracious God that He has spared you to see another birthday, and to be a witness for His love and faithfulness to the children of men, and a joy and comfort to many hearts around you; may He be pleased to give you yet many more of these returns, till perfected in His likeness He calls you to rest from your labours, and join the blessed company "over yonder." I am not going to preach to you, for if I ever did so, I was an impudent fool for my pains; for what have I to do teaching others, who have never learned my own lesson? There stands the great law of love by me unfulfilled, despite all the grace there is for that purpose,—the perfect law of perfect love to God, inspiring perfect love to all around us; that self-ignoring, self-surrendering love that, ever seeking His glory, goes forth

to all around, in the same mind that was in Him. This I know has long been yours in measure, may it yet more and more abound in you. . . . . .
Believe me, dearest Emily,<br>
Yours very affectionately,<br>
W. D. AITKEN.

The Coombe, *Tuesday Night, 22nd January, 1880.*

My very dear Friend,—Just again a few lines of love to rejoice with you, and thank God that eighty years ago He sent a little baby into the world who He Himself taught, and used for His glory. Yes, we thank Him for his birth, and for all the way He led him; the grace—His grace—He gave to him. The loss of the loved departed one was so great, that though we can bless God he is safe home, and has heard the "well done," yet oh! I cease not to long for his dear companionship and unspeakable help; and to *you* what must the blank have been and still continue to be till the bright day of re-union? How well do I remember one of his birthdays when you were away with E——; I drove to Pendeen that afternoon, and found a scene that angels must have rejoiced to witness. Your precious husband and dear good H—— engaged in the dressing-room in cutting out and distributing under-clothing to your poor friends. I need not tell you I shall (D.V.) think of you with much love and affection. On Thursday the 22nd, was the birthday of my beloved nephew, J. B——; oh! remember my brother, who is seventy-two on Thursday. . . . . . .

*April 14th, 1880.*

. . . . . . The "Brethren" are increasing here; one asked one of the St. Paul's Sunday School teachers, a working man, to come and hear the Gospel preached at St. John's Hall, telling him St. Matthew did not speak of church or chapel. The man replied, "Nor of St. John's Hall!" Mr. Morrell, who has been the past eight months at Madron, is, I hear, a converted man; the poor people say, "We need not send now for the Methodists to pray with us, for Mr. Morrell is so good as a Methody." Willie Borlase was on Friday elected member for the Eastern Division of this county, on the Liberal side. I feel almost too little interest in politics, but pray much for them; but England has had her day, and "would not."

The Coombe, *November 8th, 1882.*

My dear Mrs. Aitken,—Your card I received this morning; (D.V.) I shall be very pleased to see Dr. Nankivell on Sunday by first train, and I hope he will sleep here that night, and as many more as will suit him. I shall be much obliged if you would send me a post card, for as the upper part of the house is rarely inhabited I like a good fire to air and warm the room, and would rather prepare it before Sunday. I was naughty enough to read on your card the line you crossed out;—woman's curiosity! I should be very glad to go to Pendeen with Dr. Nankivell, but I fear I might shorten his stay there, as I require to be at home by half-past two for my Sunday afternoon gathering. We have had rough, wet weather. I am looking forward to have tolerable accounts of you. . . . .

L——, our old coachman, was converted last week; thank God in his case there was such a blessed breaking down; he seemed to want words bad enough to apply to his past life. One of his prayers I so liked: "I came to Thee in fear and in times of difficulty, but never from love." Whilst thanking for temporal blessings last Saturday he was able to praise God for his salvation. He is a very superior man, one who must consider every step before he took it; he often asked me, "Can an old sinner, a dead tree of seventy-seven, be saved?" I think inflammation of the eye, which I fear will continue dark, has been the means God has used. I saw old D—— at the Workhouse last week; he was looking so nice and well, had just returned from Pendeen, where he had been to the Feast; he told me he had been to church, and it was crowded in the evening; Mr. Meeres preached. D—— said he was very comfortable in the Union; the old woman, who is in bed, told me she was seeking God. . . . . .

With much love I remain, dear Mrs. Aitken,
Your very affectionate
E. B. B.

This is the last of Emily Bolitho's letters to Mr. and Mrs. Aitken; we now turn back to her correspondence with other friends, commencing about 1869.

## CHAPTER III.

### Letters to Friends.

(1869—1884.)

To Miss Powell, on Consecration of St. Paul's—On Captain Bedford's death—Easter, 1869, Rev. A. Mills's sermon—Watch-night Service, 1872—Death of Louie Wright—Rev. R. Aitken's death and funeral—Confirmation at Penzance—Christmas—Letters to Mr. Elwin—To Rev. G. Fenton—To Miss Fenton—To Rev. G. Savage—To Miss Haydon—To Miss M. E. Tregelles—To Miss Emma Stevens—To Miss M. Tyacke, on death of Lizzie Marks.

*S. Thomas's Day (1869 ?).*

My dearest Miss Powell,—. . . I have had such quiet evenings this Advent season, and so enjoyed them. I remember your saying to me that if I did not get to St. Paul's "the manna would fall at "The Coombe." I do so want to "rest in the Lord," and not always "asking." I see more and more it is wanting to bring something to Him, and that in others I so clearly see, it is wonderful I so cling to it myself. M. B—— said to me yesterday, "I am sure you and I ought to go to church to-day, for I call it "*our day*." How strange the collect is,—Thomas' unbelief allowed for the confirmation of our faith. I am sure I have often had to bless God for the teaching and the acknowledging of "My Lord and my God." I suppose we all know it sometimes with some measure of clinging power. I made his character my teaching at the school last night; three weeks before we had had St. Andrew, and his glorious uncompromising decision,—" There are diversities of gifts, but the same Spirit." Mr. Aitken was very excellent last Sunday, almost too encouraging as to past failure. . . . . .

The Coombe, September, 1867.

My dear Miss Powell,—For days I have been intending to write to you, but have not accomplished it, so whilst eating my breakfast I shall begin a chat. I conclude we shall soon be seeing you back, as the Lizard party (D.V.) return on Tuesday. I ho hope Mr. Fenton may be able to stay here a little time before he goes to Malvern; I do long to hear him read again, and still more to see and hear him once more in the pulpit. Will you be at home by the 25th? as on that day the church is to be consecrated. Mrs. B—— and Mr. R—— wish the present hymn book to be exchanged for "Ancient and Modern;" but though of course had A. and M. been used when we had our Hymnal, it would have been desirable to have one in such general use, yet I shall be sorry now to give up our beloved book; but of course we must submit to authority. The repeating the Thanksgiving Prayer, too, is wished to be given up; the choir are silent at that time. I allow this has grieved me; and I hear the evening Communion is intended to be given up. I feel our beloved St. Paul's has seen its best days as far as man goes, but oh! may the Lord Himself be very gracious, and visit, aye, abide with us by His own Blessed Presence; and oh! may many who have met together there meet in His House above together to praise and adore Him for ever. I cannot quite make out Mr.——. I do think that before God he is most sincere, and that he lives much in His presence; I am a very poor judge of people's character, but my own idea is that he has not very much sympathy. I don't think he can know the meaning of unbelief and doubts; in fact, he makes faith such a very simple thing. Now we have heard-salvation made simple, but the act of faith to me has never been easy. I really think he makes it so simple that people cannot understand him; I feel there is far more power in his prayers than in his sermons, but I do believe he is most anxious to *please God* and to walk humbly before Him, and to live and work for Him; and we must pray on and trust in God Who has indeed loaded us with benefits. Mr. Savage gave us deep teaching on Sunday evening from the Epistle: "God forbid that I should glory," etc., etc. He did lay us low, and show us ourselves. At the prayer-meeting on Monday he spoke on the Gospel, from the words "Ye cannot serve two Masters," etc. It was very powerful, and H—— took it up as he does so well, and prayed so earnestly "Lord make us *lovely;* we want to be lovely, for Thou art lovely; and we want to be like Thee, and that the world may see Thy loveliness reflected in us." I longed to shout "Amen, Amen."

I have been spending ten days at Torquay with W—— and K——, and their three eldest girls. I was there one Sunday, and really grieve that in that large and important place the Gospel Trumpet should, to say the least, be sounded so uncertainly. The high church very high and lifeless, and the low very low and sleepy. Oh! what manner of persons ought *we* to be who have indeed had "Line upon line," etc. I grieve over the little fruit the blessed teaching I have had has brought forth in me; the Lord might well be weary of me, but He is merciful, and gracious, and so long-suffering. . . . . .

My dear Miss Powell,—. . . . . . . That verse, "Be not high-minded, but fear," is constantly ringing in my ears; the people here seem very ready to help. I trust as it were some "cups of cold water" may by our instrumentality be given to these poor perishing ones, and that some, too, can look to One Who saves to the very uttermost.

M. T—— is spending this week with me; she is not very strong, but she is so whole-hearted that of course God uses and blesses her as He ever will those who honour Him. A week ago she was sent for to visit a sick girl; some years ago she saw her in a farm-yard, seemingly as miserable as the beasts she attended to, so untidy in her person, and so utterly ignorant, she could not read. M—— spoke to her, and gave her an adult spelling book, and occasionally went to the farm to give her a lesson; I must tell you she has only one eye, and the other so weak she could not fix it long. Well, for some years M—— quite lost sight of her, till she was called last week to see her on her sick bed; she found her so happy and thankful in the midst of much poverty and outward discomforts. For three years she has been converted; she told M—— that she was the first who ever spoke to her about her soul, and that her words had told; indeed that every one who had spoken to her she had treasured what they had said, and it had all told at last. She felt she wanted a Saviour. She had to leave service, and attend on her dying mother who was very happy in God; she longed to be like her; and one day when blowing the fire she saw one tiny spark, and she felt she could not willingly put that out, and so with her soul, so she fell on her knees and asked God to kindle a flame in her soul; and soon after she found peace. Now she delights to spell over texts, does not like stories, but is constantly reading "Mother's chapters." . . . . . .

Now, before I go to bed, for a little bright anecdote of one of M. T——'s old friends: this old man is between seventy and eighty, and lived quite a careless life, *very harmless*, far removed from any place of worship; if he ever favoured one, it was the Baptist chapel, at Helston. About two months since he was talking to a man whose dog was worrying a poor cat, and the owner would not call the dog off; this made Uncle S—— very angry, and he got into a great rage, and swore dreadfully at the man. When he went into his cottage he felt greatly shocked and horror-struck that an old man should have so given way to passion; in agony he threw himself on his knees and cried for mercy. The devil taunted him with his sin, and told him he had better destroy himself; but a Stronger than the "strong man" had come, and the old man never rested, and two days after found peace. A fortnight passed, and he had a seizure; he has lost the use of his limbs, but his intellect is perfectly good, and he is so happy in his soul and lost in wonder at God's goodness to him. M. T—— visited him last week, and told him about the Israelites putting the blood on the doors, etc. "Yes," said the old man, "I see the Blood must be put on our hearts!"

. . . . . Love for all, from your affectionate and sleepy

E. B. B.

My dear Miss Powell,—. . . . . I met with an interesting girl last week; she came to see me about a book. She has been some months in Penzance; her father a retired Independent minister, with lung disease. The girl too, exceedingly delicate, and I should say clever and well-educated; she had *heard* a great deal *about* religion, high doctrines, high professions, theological discussions; indeed the skeleton was well developed, but the breath of the Spirit had not entered into it. Well, she tried in vain to find life and reality; she went from pillar to post in search of it, but all in vain. Church and chapel did not satisfy, then the Roman Catholics, but they, too, disappointed; but, bless God, though she gave Him up, He was still the Good Shepherd seeking her. She came to lodge at Mrs. V——'s, and Anne V—— persuaded her to go to St. Paul's last Whit-Sunday; old Mr. Aitken preached. She said rather unwillingly she went, neither did the prayers nor the preaching strike her, till suddenly she felt "he is real, it is real what he says;" she felt struck. Then too, she saw Anne V——'s consistent life, and felt "that too is real." One evening she went to St. Paul's, and Robert Aitken very plainly put the way of salvation before us. She said, "I felt it was true; I bowed my head, and yielded myself up there and then;" she seems most satisfactory. She has once been to the Holy Communion, and says it was "indeed a Feast," and hopes to be there on Sunday. To-day I went to 6, Redinnick place, to see Mrs. P——'s son; he is hopelessly ill, discharged from St. Mary's Hospital incurable; the disease is internal and external too, and his sufferings very great, though I expect he may live some time. He is not converted; lately he has been able to get out very little. Of course M. A—— was full of you all; the youngest son when he comes home is to be "put" to write to you. The little girls still ask "when the train is coming that will bring Miss Gregory back." Now I think I have given

you a long letter,—a book. I wonder when we shall see J——;
I hope he will come here. . . . . .

*Monday Morning, March 3rd, 1868.*

My very dear Miss P——, Last week I fully intended to have written and told you of the rapidly-increasing and hopeless illness of our dear friend, Captain Bedford, but I really was not able to do so; now I just write a line to tell you that he "fell asleep" yesterday, at 12.40 p.m. From Thursday he was much worse; on Saturday was very restless, did not see, and was seldom sensible. The distressing restlessness continued till within an hour of his death, and now "all is over,—the pain, the sorrows." He often mentioned your name and spoke of your hymns, indeed I believe he loved and valued you very much. Last Tuesday again I was there at the Communion; he seemed much to enjoy and to enter into the service. Poor dear ——, the loss to him will be terrible! may the Lord comfort him, by revealing Himself to him. Oh! may this death be used in His hands as the means of bringing life. Poor dear M——, what a blow to her it will be! indeed, so many will greatly miss him; he is to be buried at St. Mary's, and ere I close this I will try to ascertain the day and time. His niece, F. B——, was buried at St. Mary's the day you came to Penzance. On Thursday night he said, "I have been there; don't weep for them; for they (meaning dear F—— and J——) are there; I am going to them, and you must come."

Tuesday morning. I continued this letter yesterday evening and intended to have sent it by first post to-day, but I was so poorly I could not sit up, so just conclude it now. I fancy between ten and eleven will be the time for the funeral on Friday. . . . . .

Do pray much that God's spirit and blessing may rest on a Mr. Perry; he is to be ordained priest on Sunday. . . . . .

The Coombe, *Easter Tuesday, 1869.*

My very dear Friend,—I have not forgotten you at this Holy Season, and trust that much of His Presence has been experienced by you, that your heart has burned within you when He has Himself talked with you through His Word. May we all know more and more of death, buried, and resurrection life with and from Him. Glory be to Him, He has overcome the sharpness of death, and has opened the kingdom of heaven to all believers. I had not much joy, nor had I strength of mind nor body for all I could have desired, but bless God I knew more than usual of quiet hanging on Him, and of receiving from Him many precious crumbs, aye, sometimes more than crumbs. He gives as we can bear, and as we will put forth faith to draw from His inexhaustible fulness. I was at church once each day last week. I like to assemble in God's house, but I feel I get most "good" alone, and many hours did I enjoy at The Coombe, reading, and meditating on His Word and work. . . . . .

We had no service at St. Paul's except on Tuesday and Thursday evenings, and of course twice on Good Friday. I much liked one sermon I heard at St. Mary's from Mr. Mills, of St. Erth; it helped me, and made me understand as I never had before that "God continued holy," and we must ever cling to that fact, though we, too, may cry like David in the night season, and He seem to hear not; there were many nice thoughts in that sermon. R. Aitken preached one day; it was very interesting and true and practical, but I think he might have said more. He drew such a vivid picture of the wheat being separated from the chaff, and the heavier and more valuable grain being caused to remain by the sieve being so fine that nothing but the smaller grain could pass through. It was so full of teaching;—yes, it is being sifted and searched through and through that we all need. Mr. Aitken has given us one or two masterly sermons lately; so beautiful on Good Friday evening, on His blotting out the hand-writing and triumphing over it, etc.; but the last few months he has not been well. . . .

*The Coombe, June 27th, 1870.*

My dearest Miss Powell,—From a letter from your brother, and also from Mr. Fenton, I have not had as good accounts of your health as I could have wished for, and I have been intending ere this to enquire for you, but positively these long summer days seem far shorter than those of winter, and nothing is done. I have had friends staying with me, and though not over polite or attentive to them, still it has all left less time for letter writing; but now I have curtailed my afternoon rest on the sofa, and hope to have an undisturbed little chat with you till 5.20, when I have told Anne to bring me some tea prior to my intended drive to Pendeen. I know you will be thankful to hear our dear valued friend, Mr. Aitken, goes on most favourably; I saw him last Tuesday, that was the first time he was out, and I sat with him for an hour in the front of the vicarage; he did so enjoy the bright sunshine and fine fresh air. He was looking very ill, quite a weak old man, and seemed glad to have my arm, and I pleased to be able to help him; and I hope very thankful to have been able to send him a few little nice things. The fever which has been so general and fatal in the parish has, I trust, much abated. Mr. Aitken had taken forty funerals in less than three months, and to his feeling heart this alone was a severe strain. I trust now in God's good providence he may soon recover. Two strangers who have been visiting here have taken the church during his illness. Robert has been there almost daily. His sermons the last few weeks have been most interesting, impressive, and instructive, on the teaching of the first Sunday lessons; so earnest on Joshua telling Israel of what God had done for them, and chosen them, though so little for such a great purpose, and showing that every step of the journey from Jordan to Jerusalem must be warfare and opposition; but so encouraging that we the little ones should chase the thousands and put the ten thousands to flight, for the Lord fought for us, and that we must put our feet on the necks of the five kings. Then yesterday a sad picture of God's people *sold* into the hands of the King of Canaan with his nine hundred chariots, and his mighty and long-continued oppression; they cry to the Lord in their distress, and He hears and delivers; but no honour to Israel, Sisera sold into the hands of a woman. I never thought so much before of the honourable position,—Zebulon and Napthali both jeoparded their lives unto the death. We had the same subject for the three sermons, as, after full service and a sermon of half-an-hour, Mr. Aitken went to the Fairfield and had an hour-and-a-half service there, and preached; Sisera's mother's anxiety gave the key-note. Very solemn and earnest it was, and well attended and very orderly; a few roughs there, and many in our congregation who have so often hardened their necks. I trust some seed may have been received into honest hearts that may bring forth fruit. Did you see a little remark in the "Revival" some months ago, of a lady at Round Lake Camp Meeting? She said at the breakfast she "had been walking in the woods, and delighted to see all

L

the green things so refreshed and fragrant from the effects of heavy dew, but one plant looked dry and withered and without moisture, caused by a cobweb being over it that took off the dew from the plant; and so if any webs of our own weaving cover our soul, the dew of God's spirit *cannot* descend and revive and refresh us." Is it not a nice thought? And I will tell you another too. Last week, at Pendeen, a poor butterfly was for a long time buzzing and beating about on the window, trying in vain to get free; at last it fell down as if dead on the ledge close to the open part, and in a moment it was in *full liberty*. "Leave off desire and you shall find rest," says Fénélon; and so when we relinquish our own fleshly strivings and sink into and upon Him, we too shall find rest. It is easy to write all this, but oh! to be it. . . . . .

*The Coombe, 1871.*

My very dear Miss Powell,—Yesterday and to-day I intended to have called on you, but the weather has prevented me; it is indeed cold and dismal, and I should greatly value you as my fire-side companion, but oh, what a mercy to have a fire-side! I fear there is terrible want on every side. I cannot tell you how much I miss you; Ann[1] was quite tender in her attentions; she has placed the quilt you had, over me the last two nights; she talks of you several times a day, and says she never liked any visitor in the house here as much, adding, she was afraid sometimes you were going to speak to her; so perhaps, as God has given you such favour in her eyes, the " bread you have cast on the waters may return after many days." I was made very thankful last night by that sick man "Eddy" realizing Jesus as his Saviour; when I saw him I

---

1 Her faithful servant, who lived with her thirty-two years.

thought him softened, and he often earnestly said "Lord, have mercy upon me." Whilst I was praying he burst out into such quiet praise; he is a reserved, silent man, but it was all so real; his closed eyes, with tears running down his cheeks, and his earnestly clasped hands, and the unceasing "Glory be to God." I shall not soon forget the happy scene; he says H—— visited him on Thursday, and he got a little measure of light. I have seen him again this morning; he seems clear, and so quietly happy,—praise *flowing* so naturally from his lips; I am very thankful; and as he is much better, it shows it is not fear of death that has driven him to Jesus. . . . . .

Lariggan, *January 5th, 1872.*

My very dear Miss Powell,—It is nearly time to go to bed, but I will just have a few words with you before I go upstairs, to thank you for your kind letter, and pretty enclosures. I have an idea of sending the little picture to a poor inmate of the Lunatic Asylum. Her case is a strange one: about a year ago I took my favourite little picture—"The Good Shepherd taking the sheep out of the thorns"—to a poor old woman, and telling her what it taught us. I had almost forgotten the circumstance, till a few months since a poor woman came up to me in the street, the daughter of the old woman, and mentioned it, adding, "I never forgot it, and thought I would come to Jesus like that; and I looked up and gave myself to Him, and He has made me happy." A few days after she lost her senses, and is now a quiet but hopeless lunatic; her husband visited her last week, and she was so pleased to hear I had enquired for her, and laughed so much about it, adding to the nurse, "She is a bigger woman than you, nurse." But what a long digression! Give my very kind Christian regards to your dear mother; I sometimes envy you having such a treasure as a parent, and trust yours may yet be spared to you. May the year on which we have entered be one of much progress, as Wesley says:—

> "Deeper sink, and higher rise,
> And to perfection grow."

We had our usual Sunday and Christmas Day services, and on Christmas and on New Year's Eve we had Watch-night services with celebrations of the Holy Communion; these I much enjoyed, and treated myself to a close carriage both of these nights, as I had a cold and did not expose myself much to the night air at that time. The church was very prettily decorated, and my six Borlase nieces took very much trouble about it the previous week. Mr. Aitken has had a very bad cold and cough the last month, and Mr. L—— is not strong; he has only preached once,—it was very good but rather too formal, but I like his prayers, and *he is* a good man.

*Feast of the Epiphany.*

Thus far I wrote on Thursday but had not time to finish it, and now we are soon going to church. May the True Star, God the Holy Ghost, guide us every moment, and may we, obediently following His guidance, see Jesus, and yield up willingly all to Him,—"All things come of Thee, and of Thine own do I give unto Thee." . . . . .

But I must conclude. I was at Pendeen on Thursday; Mr. Aitken invited to conduct a mission at Sheffield in February. And now with kind remembrances and every good wish for your mother and family, and with very much of love for yourself,

I remain, dear Miss Powell,

Your very loving

E. B. B.

The Coombe, *Thursday, February 22nd, 1872.*

My very dear Miss Powell,—I fancy I have long been in your debt, but it is useless to promise to do better for the future, for indeed my arm aches so with my little amount of writing, that I fear its powers will lessen rather than increase; but I will not waste time in a useless preface. You were, I am sure, much shocked to hear of dear Louie Wright's death; for her all was bright, but she has left dear ones to mourn her great loss. I had a few lines from her dear mother this week, and I see the *Daphne* is to come to England to bring back Lord Mayo's body, so Edmund Nankivell will see his changed home and dear children before he expected. I am, for Mrs. Wright's sake, glad of this; I hope she will soon leave that lonely place; I wish she might return to Bournemouth, or still rather to Penzance. Eight years to-day since dear J. B—— was called away, I trust, to be for ever with the Lord he loved. How are you, dear Miss Powell? I wonder if you will meet Mr. Aitken; I fancy he is at Sheffield this week. Mr. Lomax set off to-day to join him; *entre nous* I think he had better have remained to help Robert, who is very far from well; he has been preaching such deep, interesting, and spiritual sermons since his illness. . . . . .

We have had a great loss this week, as Captain Cay has taken command of the *Vulture*, and on Monday is to sail from Sheerness to the Persian Gulf. Poor dear Mrs. Cay! indeed for both of them it is a deep, though necessary, trial. We had last Sunday evening such a very touching season at the Communion; that night five years you and dear Miss Fenton were there. Mr. Aitken had the hymn sung, "Yes we part, but not for ever," and he prayed such a touching extempore prayer; the next morning he and I were at the station to see him off, and to bring poor Mrs. Cay home. She went to his house, and we had a little prayer there before I set her on her way home through the Treneere fields; they live now just opposite Wesley Rock chapel. I expect a visit from M. T—— soon, and I hope we shall have a profitable time together. . . . . .

I am reading the life of Alexander Dallis; it is interesting, but so terribly spun out. . . . . .

I have very little opinion of death-bed conversions, but still, bless God, He can and does save to the uttermost, and by all means too. An instance of this happened here a few weeks ago. A vessel was wrecked; all saved but one seaman and the captain's wife and two children. He escaped with his child fastened round him, but the waves were too strong for his young life, and when the father got to shore his boy's lifeless body was still clinging to him; it seems the wife was a converted woman, and he had laughed at her when she knelt in prayer with her children. He came to Penzance desolate, wife and two children (he had no more) gone, and all his property was in the ship that was a total wreck, but God found him: "To be lost is to be loved." Mr. M—— brought him to the Wesleyan chapel, and there, after much prayer with and for him, he too prayed to One Who is a prayer-hearing God, and Who heard and answered his cry. . . . . .

Oh, dear Miss Powell, how I wish you were here! How is your dear mother? Remember me most kindly to her; and how are you all going on? Do write and tell me you will come and see me. Ann and I should be so pleased. . . . . .

We have a Litany and address at noon on Wednesdays, and full service on Fridays, during Lent. The lots I could write about!—but it is getting dark, and I have some girls coming to tea; so good bye. Very much love,

Your affectionate<br>E. B. B.

The Coombe, 11 p.m., *October 22nd, 1872*.

My dear Miss Powell,—I have been at Pendeen this afternoon to see Mrs. Aitken, who returned last Thursday. Robert Aitken has been very ill,—a return of his old complaint; he is better again, and preached most wonderful sermons on Sunday, the Epistle his subject. Oh! what a picture did he draw of what a Christian soldier should be,—our high and holy and unselfish calling. I felt humbled in the very dust, "Cast down, but not in despair." It was the third Sunday, and the Holy Communion was indeed a help and refreshment. We sang the old hymn, "Soldiers of Christ arise," etc. Yesterday morning too, at the prayer-meeting, he continued the same subject;—he is a wonderful and most edifying preacher. I grieve ever that I profit so little by such deep teaching. I visit every week, and oftener if I can, a sweet invalid, a Miss Plimmer. You would like her so much; like a few others she is woefully deceived in her thoughts of me; but never mind what I am, if God lets me sometimes say a word for Him to His dear afflicted child. Angels may wonder at such a messenger being used. I visited a sick girl to-day who said to me, "You must not talk to me like that; you will make me bad, I can't be excited;" and when I asked her if I might pray, she said, "I would rather not." Poor girl, I am sure she is very ill, and certainly at present very uninteresting and unsatisfactory. May the Lord show her herself and Himself. . . . . .

I saw A. N—— last week; she lives at Hayle. Her husband has plenty of work, and they seem to be going on very comfortably; she has six children. They are both religious, and their eldest girl seems to love good things. We have very good accounts from dear M. G——; her health is so good. . . . . .

I see the old lady T—— very often. Thank God He gives me strength from day to day, but oh, how I want to know more of Him! "Thou art the Thing that I long for." . . . . .

It is getting late, and I think I must conclude my scrawl. Remember me to your dear mother and sisters, and with very much love for your very dear self,

I remain, dear Miss Powell,
Your loving
E. B. B.

The Coombe, *December 23rd, 1872.*

My very dear Miss Powell,—Appearances have decidedly been against me; but truly I can say, daily for weeks have I wished to write to you, but the time to perform the desire never has arrived. Don't for one moment think I do a great amount of work, etc., but I have so many interruptions, and though, thank God, I have a most comfortable share of health, and am surrounded by countless mercies, still I am obliged to get long rests, and my thoughts are so wandering that I find I have spent an hour on my knees or over my Bible, and I fear most of the time my heart has been far away; but excuses are vain, and I have other letters I must try to write this evening. I love to think of you, and so often want to hear you sing hymns. Do you not love that one in the Appendix, "At even, ere the sun was set?" I am so fond of it (not that my voice can manage it). I hope your dear mother is tolerable for her, and that you may have a peaceful Christmas, much of His Presence in your midst,—Himself abiding with you, and giving you all His blessing, and filling you with His fulness. The weather is very mild, and yesterday it was *most lovely*, but we have had it most unsettled, stormy, and very wet. I have a very excellent pair of thick high boots, and have been out in all weathers, and thank God thus far have been free from cold. The accounts of dear Mr. Fenton are, I do trust, really improved. Fancy his taking Evening Prayers; and what a touching season that must have been, November 23rd, when he administered the Holy Communion; I would have given much to have been there. On the whole, too, I hope dear C—— does not lose ground. . . . . .

Very much love. Your affectionate
E. B. B.

The Coombe, *July 30th, 1873.*

My very dear Miss Powell,—I have been long wishing to write to you, but for many reasons have not been able to do so, and now I feel weary and listless and equal to so little exertion of mind or body, so you must not expect anything interesting. I should much like to see you and to talk together over the subject which you may be sure is very near my heart. Thank you for your kind letter and warm sympathy. I daily seem to get more alive to the terrible loss that has fallen on us, and I cannot realize the bright "beyond;" I don't doubt God, and I know He can fill empty places, and that He is Love, and doeth all things well and for some wise purpose of His own; but still this does not lessen the fact of the, in this world, irreparable loss; personal loss and general loss,—aye, loss to those who refused to hear him and would not receive

M

the message the Master gave him to deliver for Him. The trumpet in his case gave no uncertain sound, and bless God it did not sound in vain. Many received the voice of invitation and of warning, and fled for refuge to the Ark of Safety. Oh, dear, dear Miss Powell, how shall I give him up! I knew I loved him, but never till now did I know how much. God has given me a few occasional glimpses of Himself since, but my general experience has been a chaotic void, and so insensible and dead,—nothing beyond the present, and then the crying has been most trying; I think I never shed as many tears; and that weakens and unfits me, and though the weather has not been over hot I feel it very oppressive. I want to get a practical result from this solemn call; the seeing him ever before me as I now do, and weeping for him, will not do any real good. I want to be more entirely the Lord's, and live and work for Him as I have never done, but at present all seems hedged up; do pray that He will guide and direct me. I stand too much alone; others don't understand my sorrow and the loss of one who has been as a second father, and whose house was a second home, and now in a few days all will be closed! To see the confusion and preparation for the exodus! Yesterday morning I accompanied Mr. and Mrs. Savage and their dear little boy as far as Hayle *en route* for home. Mr. Savage's last words were, 2 Corinthians, xiii., 11. He is so nice and good, and so happy and trusting;—quite refreshing to be with him. Willie[1] dined with me yesterday; dear, dear Willie! I feel proud that I once nursed him, put on leeches, etc. I cannot bear to think we shall see no more of him either; he leaves on Friday for home, he is very done up; he prayed so sweetly with me before he left yesterday,

[1] Rev. W. H. Aitken.

and thanked God for the tears of Jesus by the grave of Lazarus. I fear my writing is very indistinct, my right hand has not been quite well for months, and to-day it is more troublesome than usual. Mr. Dodge says it is rheumatic gout; it really is not much except it hinders my writing. Mrs. Aitken and dear Mrs. Macdowell go on the 7th,—the former direct to Eda,[1] and the latter to Scotland for a few weeks, and then these widowed sisters propose residing at Penmellyn with the Nankivells. Dear, dear Mrs. A. looks so old, but is so calm and precious; I felt ashamed at *her* pouring comfort into *my* ears; I hope I may say heart. She said to me last week, "I shall be a living martyr, but not without my God, not without my Saviour." Robert showed very kind feeling to me after the funeral. He has twice said to me, "I can never be to you what *he* was, but, God helping me, I will be to you all I can be." Oh, Miss Powell, it was so dreadful to go to the station and see the coffin taken out that held the precious remains! The funeral was a most trying time; oh, it was agony to see the coffin carried out of that dear church that was so identified with the precious departed! On it were placed three beautiful wreaths. The hymns were very touching. Poor dear Mr. Roe had hard, very hard work to take the service at the grave; twelve clergymen carried him: but then to come back to that empty drawing-room! that was worst of all. Mr. Williams and Mr. Drake were opposite me. Oh, the flood of memories that they brought back! The day before the funeral I was at Pendeen. I said I would be back to dinner at two o'clock; at half-past three I rushed in and ordered dinner, but Anne stopped me, saying there were three ladies in the drawing-room, adding that just before the three p.m. train came Mr. R. Aitken came

[1] Mrs. Aitken's daughter, Mrs. Nankivell.

here to know if I could receive them, and I found Mrs. and Miss Mary Harmaul and Mrs. Baxter (Lizzie Foster). Anne was most amiable and good, and they so simple and nice that I was very glad to have them. I believe they did me good. Dear Miss Powell, I think I must change the subject, though I have not much else to say. I should much like to have had Mr. Fenton, but still I was glad he decided not to come; I am sure he was not fit for it. I hope he may like Clifton, but I fear he has rather lost ground. A party of one hundred have been lunching at the Smelting Works to-day off beef-steaks dressed on the tin;—a Mechanical Engineers' Congress, some Sheffield men there. I hope your mother and sisters are pretty well; remember me to them. I must close this and go out a little, so good-bye.

'I remain, dear Miss Powell,
Your very loving friend,
E. B. B.

I am ashamed to send this but am too tired to read it over.

The Coombe, *August 16th, 1873.*

My very dear Friend,—Oh! how often during the last never-to-be-forgotten five weeks have I longed to lay my head on your dear shoulder, and that we might together weep out our souls. I dare say it has been far better that I have had few earthly helpers, and had to wait only on God. Sometimes it has been very, very dark, and then again He has given "Songs in the night;" and it has been sweet to have the loving sympathy of many dear Christian friends whose letters have en great comforts, and yours, my dear Miss Powell, was indeed sweet; God bless you for it. I ought not to arrogate all this sympathy to myself; I am but one in the mighty many who are weeping the loss of the holy dead. I am sure we all feel most *proud* and thankful that such atoms as we were allowed to know and love him, aye, and be loved by one who, as your friend Mr. Jackson said, "his majestic manhood was full of Christ." Oh! how don't I love the Master more, when it was so easy to love the dear servant?

Here I have had visitors and interruptions.

. . . . . . Was it not strange that several who assisted in bearing those precious remains to their last resting place were those who never came near him when he was alive? The Lord lay not that sin to their charge. I heard from Eda Nankivell yesterday; she gave a tolerable report of that dear bereaved wife; I think she will be quite as happy in her present position as she could possibly be. Dear Eda too wants a kind mother's care, and I think dear Mrs. Aitken may be very useful to Herbert's patients. Mary and Mr. Savage seem so nice and good, and happy in the Lord. H—— is a very pretty little boy. Dear Willie! oh, I do love him, poor dear fellow! He was very broken-hearted; he dined with me one day, and prayed so sweetly before he left. Do you know hymn 191, A. and M.? they sang it at St. Paul's the day after that never-to-be-forgotten Saturday. Oh, it was a crushing day!

I could write sheets about all the events of the past five weeks, but I am late and tired, and it is almost selfish. I think it has made me love dear Mr. Fenton more than ever; he has written me dear little letters, and quite helped me. It is yet unfixed who will have Pendeen; it is not a desirable place. The dear Roes are at Ben Rhydden, both very unwel' and in that establishment there. I never think they will remain long at the Land's End; it is too lonely and too wild a place for either of those nervous sensitive creatures; they are very dear warm-hearted people, and I should greatly miss them. We are now all very anxious about Elizabeth Carne, she is most seriously ill; first low fever, then inflammation of the lungs. They feared this might prove fatal, but it has in a great measure been subdued, but now prolonged gastric fever is running its course, and she is certainly not improving; her mind is most peaceful. Much prayer is ascending for her that God may see fit to spare her very valuable and useful life.

I have been many hours this week with a dying man. To me the case was most unsatisfactory. Do you remember that Gulval Mrs. R——? it is her husband; he died yesterday morning, leaving four children. I hope it may decide the wife; she has had impressions, but it was a solemn death-bed, and I trust I may learn some lessons from it. I have been anxious about a dying girl of twenty; she was an old school girl and is married, and come home to die; her infant has died this week. She has seemed so insensible and drowsy, but when I saw her this morning her bright smile and changed face told its own tale. Bless God! she can now trust her Saviour.

I get weekly letters from M. T——; she is deeply interested and I think a little puzzled herself about P. Smith's teaching, "They that can receive the Gift let them receive it;" but I cannot entirely think with them, though I long for more faith, or rather can say with David, "Thou art the Thing that I long for;" and His Word says, "He will fulfil the desire of them that fear Him." Sure I am, nothing but Himself can satisfy. But it is past eleven, and I must prepare for bed. I hope you are tolerable, and your mother and sisters pretty well; remember me to them. How does your brother's wife go on?

Very much love, I remain,<br>
My very dear Miss Powell,<br>
Your very loving<br>
E. B. B.

The Coombe, *October, 1874.*

My dear Miss Powell,— . . . . . I want more entirely to sit under "His Shadow with great delight," and find "His fruit sweet to my taste." I don't know this as I increasingly long to do, but I do more and more know that nothing else satisfies, and that all else disappoints. Those lines are so constantly in my mind,—

" Alone who has Thee in his heart,<br>
Knows, Love of Jesus, what Thou art."

It is this experience I long for, and then all yearning and craving for, and being disappointed in, human love, will take such a subordinate place; but I cannot tell why I am writing all this, and my aching arm and side make me feel I must soon put it away to rest. I do think from your letters that you must be better, and I hear you are not supposed to reap the full benefit of German waters, baths, etc., till some months after; I hope this may be your case. I very often think of you all; I was thinking this afternoon how nice it would be to have Aunt Gee Gee here, and dear Mary P——, if they had come as they had intended. I so much prefer autumn to spring visitors, but then every day brings far too much work and interruptions to give me time to be polite to visitors; the days fly in a most unaccountable manner, and yet time is such a very solemn talent.

I had on the whole a happy birthday; I had a nice long quiet before breakfast, and then visited as usual Mrs. Hall and Mrs. Vibert before church. Robert's sermon very nice on "His loving correction has made me glad," etc.; then, a most blessed Communion. After dinner, the school-room; that was a trying and solemn time; our last gathering there, as all the buildings and cottages from Chyandour bridge to the Station on the sea-side are taking down, to make room for railway buildings. Twenty-one families have taken their departure from the village. Well, I did and do greatly feel the giving up of that room, where for thirty years we have had the school, and where for seventeen I have had my classes; "the gourd" was not beautiful, but it was often a blessed shelter and over-shadowing. Bless God! I do hope it was the birthplace of some souls. L. A—— amongst the number; dear old Jimmy Donnithorne dearly loved the little "mittins" in that "upper chamber;" dear Mr. Aitken and dear Mr. Grant had spoken there. I tried to be very brave; I scarcely know our future, but suppose the mission-room the other side of the village will be our meeting place; but as the carpenter told me this afternoon he should not unroof the school-room for a few days, I shall (D.V.) cling to the old ship another Sunday. Taylor was there on Sunday, and at church also. . . . . .

*The Coombe, 1875.*

My dear Miss Powell,—I hope you are all tolerable, and your dear mother comfortable. I think often of you, and should greatly like a chat with you, and wish you could sing sweet hymns to me.

There was a Confirmation here last week,—fourteen from St. Paul's. One woman found peace as the Bishop put his hands on her head; she is a very respectable steady woman of thirty, and had long been troubled about her soul. She said to Miss Harvey, "I knew the Bishop's hands could do no good, but I knew it was an act of obedience;" if ever you see Mr. J——, tell him this.

A poor fisherman, one of Mr. Roe's people—"Uncle Peter" is his name in the Cove where he is well known—was praying the other day, and used the following expression, "Father, I 'spose a jewel is something very fine; I don't know that I ever seed one, but Thou hast spoke about them, so they must be precious." This was as well as I can remember, but I thought it was a sweet remark. . . . . .

The Coombe, November 6th, 1876.

My dearest Miss Powell,—I very often think of you and wish to write to you, but each day brings its work or interruptions, and night often finds me too weary to use my pen. I think and hope it is a sort of neuralgia that gives pain and weakness in my right arm and shoulder and that side of the chest. Thank God, thus far all seems satisfactory the *other side*.[1] I trust you are tolerably well; I know you suffer from rheumatism. How true and how beautiful is that hymn,—"At even, ere the sun was set;" I should like to hear you sing it. . . . . .

I am a very stupid writer, but I should like a long chat with you. St. Paul's is now without a pastor; I trust you pray

---

[1] On 31st March, 1875, she had undergone an operation for tumour in the left side. She had prepared for it most bravely and calmly, desiring to have it done in her own house and by her own doctors, and to have no one else with her but her brother and her servant Anne. The latter said the only fear she expressed beforehand was lest she should say anything wrong when under chloroform. "I do pray that I may not," she said; and Anne was able to re-assure afterwards that she had sung "Safe in the arms of Jesus" the whole time, so that even in unconsciousness the Name dearest to her heart was on her lips.

for us. Mr. Aitken has been gone four weeks; so far we have been nicely cared for. Mr. Andrewes we liked so very much; he has sole charge of Paul, and is doing work there which I believe God is blessing; he kindly comes to us on Tuesday evening, and at his own request takes the Wednesday afternoon bible-class which is now assembled at Miss Haydon's, and reminds us much of the past happy days. All the classes have increased the last few months. Oh! may the Lord Himself come down as "rain on the mown grass." I think we are like weaned children, and He alone can provide for or comfort us; prayer seems our position, and may "He fulfil the desire of them who fear Him.". . . . .

The Coombe, *December 23rd, 1876.*

My very dear Friend,—It seems long since I have had a talk with you; every day brings its full share of work or interruption, and night overtakes me with little accomplished. My powers of mind and body are becoming more feeble; the "windows darken," but still I get on without artificial help; "the grinders" are less than "few," as *all* I possess are supplied by Mr. Magor; but thank God for the countless mercies I possess, and the most comfortable share of strength He gives me. I often think of you, and should greatly enjoy a talk with you, but this busy week I can even with my pen only give you a few kind words, to convey love and every Christian wish at this holy season, that the Lord may make you very happy in close communion with Himself. May He, "the Bread of Life," feed us at Bethlehem, and show us much of "the mystery of godliness," in the person of the Lord Jesus. We have together here often spent this holy happy season, and when the Master comes may it be joyfully to rise up to meet

Him Whom our souls love. The past has been a very trying year to me, and I have indeed had to sorrow with many dear bereaved ones.

St. Paul's is still without a settled pastor, but we have a very good preacher there now, a Mr. Thistleton from Dublin. Poor Mrs. B—— still goes on, her sufferings so very great; she rests on the Lord, but it is still a struggle.

It is time to go to bed, and my pen will not write, so with every fond loving wish

I remain, dear Miss Powell,
Your very affectionate
E. B. B.

P.S.—I hope you are tolerable, and your dear mother and sisters also; remember me most kindly to them, and will you forward the enclosed to your brother. The Lord bless thee, dear friend; I should like to hear thy dear voice.

The Coombe, *Christmas, 1877.*

My dearest Miss Powell,—This blessed season must not pass without a few words of love to send you and yours every kind wish; may yours be the Christian's joy, "too deep to be noisy, too full to be frothy." If He gives peace, none can make war; He sits above every water flood, and *remaineth* a King for ever. I do trust we may both be much in spirit at Bethlehem, and have such glimpses by faith of "the King of Glory," that, like the happy shepherds, we may return to our various duties rejoicing; and may He be our Strength in all that is before us in the untried future. I got a letter from Mrs. Aitken on Tuesday which led me to fear our dearly-loved and deeply-valued friend Mr. Fenton was really passing away;

but to-day the report from his dear sister was far more hopeful, and I do trust for the sake of his dear family he may yet continue, and though his *seen* work in God's vineyard is not much, yet the prayers he offers and the tracts he sends may be blessings to many. . . . . .

My dear Mr. Elwin,[1]—For weeks I have heen hoping to hear from Mary; I should have written before but am ignorant of your address, as you belong to the wandering tribes; but I trust wherever you are God is giving you work and blessing. I see from "The Revival" that you are returned from Lancashire, and after all the deeply interesting scenes you have witnessed my stories may be tame; but as I find you make use of them, I who am such an idler and live for so little purpose, gladly send you a few little outlines that you may fill up. I don't see "The London Messenger," but was rather amused a month ago to find the story about feeding the ants had got in it. I said to the person that mentioned it (Trembath, Mr. Smith's Scripture Reader) "You must have got that from 'The London Messenger,' as the original letter came to Mr. Fenton." I found I was right in my guess. Have you heard the story of a little girl who was learning to read, and *fortunately* did not divide her letters? Her father was a sceptic. An old friend of his was coming to sleep at his house; he was the deputation for a missionary meeting that was to be held in the town. Before he came, his intended host, being very open in his denial of a God, printed on a card, intending to hang it in his room, "God is nowhere." He called his little girl and told her to read it, and she spelt letter after letter "God is

---

[1] Mr. Elwin married her cousin, Miss Mary Harris.

*now here.*" He said "That is wrong, read it again;" but One Who takes the weak things of this world to confound the wise again directed those lisping lips, and again she read "God is *now here.*" (Oh, what a difference does one letter make!) "You are wrong," said the father. "No," said the child; "I know it is right, for mamma said 'God is everywhere.'" This simple truth was the arrow that God in love used to enter in and work life in that unbeliever's soul. It is past eleven p.m., and I must go to bed, but first I will just tell you a little word I heard to-day. I dare say you have heard it before. A minister (may I say a clergyman? for I believe it was) was visiting the dying-bed of an old woman. He said to her, "You are sinking fast." Turning her earnest dying eyes on him she said, "No, bless God, I am not sinking, I am on the Rock, and That never can sink; Its foundation is sure, and on It I am resting, and It bears me up above all the billows." I asked a man a few weeks since, how long he had known the Lord? He replied, "twenty years nearly, and I found God when a sailor on board a man-of-war. We were five hundred men, all quite careless and prayerless; we took a seaman on board in the Mediterranean, and he seemed so different from all the others that I could not help observing him; he was always most punctual at his duties. I often found him at night on his knees; he was the laughing-stock of the whole crew. One day I remarked to some others, "What do you see in that man that you so laugh at and torment him? "Do you mean to turn Methodist too?" was the reply I got. "I don't know if he be a Methodist or what he is, but I wish I was like him." From that day I began to pray. I was perfectly ignorant of the way of salvation, but still at night I would creep out of my bed and kneel behind a gun and pray; at last I could bear it no longer, and I sought the Christian sailor and told him my case, and that observing his conduct had made a deep impression on me, and he told me of Jesus, and of the way of access to the Father by Him. . . . . .

*The Coombe, Easter Monday, 9.30 a.m., 1871.*

My dear Mr. Fenton,—I am just returned from church, where we have had a most wonderfully political sermon from R. Aitken,—the angel passing over the sprinkled houses his supposed text. I do trust a very big cloud of heartfelt praise has ascended to-day. Oh! for more of the prayer of faith for our Prince's soul. Dr. Gull told a gentleman who told T—— that he had never witnessed such a case; that for ten hours he held the sufferer in his arms, and believes if he had changed his position the breath would have gone. I went to St. Mary's this morning, and had a very nice, well-conducted simple service; the choir, but no organ. The lessons—Hezekiah and nobleman's son—so suitable; there was no sermon, but the Communion; not more than thirty received. The grand choral service was at two; no end of Odd and even Fellows, corporation, coast-guard, life-boat's crew, etc., etc., with all their ensigns, rifle corps. . . . . .

*The Coombe, Easter Monday, 9.30 p.m.*

My dear Mr. Fenton,—The last hour I have been enjoying perfect quiet in the dark on the sofa. I have been remembering you and yours as I do more than once each day, and now I will have a little talk with you, but I get almost daily less inclined to write letters. In many respects I am wonderfully well and strong, but in others I shrink from all exertion, and feel as if to lie on the sofa with closed eyes was the only desirable occupation; and I really do think I am old! and when yesterday I remembered the fact that Easter Day, 1836, was the time of my first Communion, I did feel surprised at the rapid flight of time, and deep sorrow that my life has been such a failure, and so unsatisfactory. Oh! if He spares my life may I yet bring forth more fruit in my age; but I so often feel I have not begun really to live. Thank you for the stamps; I scarcely feel I ought to keep them, as you sent me a double supply at Christmas, or rather told me to keep those that were intended for the Newlyn man, who we hope has the place beside "the River," and that he does sing of salvation for ever and ever. . . . . .

I do hope you are better again, and able in some measure to enjoy the dear young people; I have thought so very much of you during Holy Week, and the happy holy seasons we have had together. . . . . .

. . . . . . We had a very nice Holy Week,—I mean its services, etc. I don't like a Mr.—— who most kindly has helped Mr. Aitken; he is a very tiresome reader, but of that I do not so much complain; but when he preaches the Bloodless Sacrifice, the Life, the Pattern, etc., I feel as if I ought not to sit still; for though all is true as far as the Life of our Lord being the perfect Example, still Romans iii., 25, tells what is needed first; but I wonder Robert is able to go on as he has done night after night. He had two services in the church on Monday, addresses at each; and after every evening service, a prayer-meeting in the church. On Wednesday the church was open all day for prayer. Well, now I remember what till now I had quite forgotten, that I had written to you last week; well, now I must go on—Wednesday I did enjoy;

the silent time for prayer in the church was blessed; at noon Mr. Aitken was there, and prayed. . . . . . After the meeting Mrs. Legge and I went into the church, and there I found Miss T——, who for days had been seeking on her knees alone in the church. I went and knelt beside her, and God let me help her a little, and she was able to trust her Saviour; then after a time Mrs. Boase and Miss Harvey came into the church; we had a little singing and praising God together, and it was so sweet to watch the smile of settled peace *settling* on her face. I found Psalm xl., 2, very helping; her mother too has been very religious, but only last week found rest in Christ; they have been Wesleyans. Thursday evening we had a most interesting service, so many new communicants, indeed one hundred and ten received. On Friday night two found peace in the church. . . . . . After every service Robert gave a long and stirring address in the school-room on the passage through the Red Sea; I should think about one hundred people in the room. We had a little service in church at noon to-day, but only forty there; it was so wet, and the rain prevented my being at the meeting this evening. . . . . .

The Coombe, *Saturday Evening, 12th July, 1873.*

My dear Mr. Fenton,—I can give you no further particulars[1] I felt this morning as if I would willingly keep you ignorant of the deep sorrow that has fallen on us, and I shrink from telegraphing, but Mr. Savage asked me to do so, and I too felt you might see it in the paper; I hope my telegram got in time to prevent that shock. I feel now "done." Dear, dear old man! how unlike the falling asleep process that we should have chosen for him. I cannot bear to think of it,

---

[1] Mr. Aitken's sudden death.

but he is "For ever with the Lord," and has pitched his tent at Home. Dear, dear Mr. Aitken, oh, how much of the last nineteen years has been identified with him! I heard the sad intelligence early this morning, and directly after breakfast went to see the railway guard, and heard the few particulars we are ever likely to have from him. The dear old man left the N——'s on Thursday at Schwalbach, and came alone (this ought not to have been allowed) to London; he took some refreshment at the station, came out, and asked for the Penzance guard; just as he reached him he fell, never spoke, drew a few breaths, and all was over. A doctor was on the platform, and the Great Physician sent His angel or came Himself and took the spirit of our beloved and justly valued friend and adviser. I get sick when I think of it. He does intend to teach me to lean only on Himself and no arm of flesh however dear. . . . . .

The Coombe, *July 14th, 1873, 11 p.m.*

My dear Miss Fenton,—Thinking it possible Mr. Fenton and M—— may have left, I write a line to you. I should be very pleased to see them, but could not urge their coming; I fear the necessary excitement, and I feel so done up myself that I shrink from the painful pleasure of performing the sacred duty that (D.V) I shall engage in on Friday next, at four p.m. John ii., 16, seems always before me. Perhaps to rouse me might be good. Oh! dear Miss Fenton, every one seems so good and resigned, and so to rejoice in his happiness. Oh, I cannot feel like that! to cry my eyes out suits me best. Oh, I long to think it is a dream! Yesterday was dreadful,—St. Paul's like a hearse and mourning coach and everything else; not a bit of stone pulpit seen; eagle, lectern, communion table, and rail covered in double-dyed black cloth—quite overdone. White played the "Dead March in Saul" twice; melancholy chants; and oh, such hymns! 191 the first—"Ye servants of the Lord." In the evening so nice,—Mr. Edmunds preached a funeral sermon, and Mr. Devenish broke down in the litany: then the evening prayer-meeting; H—— gave a sort of address; one remark was "Mr. Aitken's last word was 'Penzance!'" God said "No, not Penzance, but Paradise." He added, "many grand trains have lately left Paddington, but no train ever left Paddington station so grand as that on Friday evening, when a train of angels conveyed that happy spirit safe Home." I have been at Pendeen this evening; all very tolerable. Mrs. Aitken went into Penzance to-day, intending to go off to Paddington for a last look at the dear remains, but on her way got a letter from Willie saying it was necessary all should be closed. . . . . .

Much love, your affectionate<br>E. B. B.

The Coombe, *Saturday Morning, 1863.*

My own dearest Polly (Miss M. Tyacke),—I do like to have a weekly chat with you dear, but oh, time! time! the day is gone almost before it seems begun, and certainly nothing seems done. Oh, this fact should keep down self-satisfaction well.

*Monday Morning.*

You see by these dates I have not forgotten you, but oh! the multiplicity of things that come after me to do, and thank God He tells me to-day that "without Him we can do nothing." I received your letter last night; thank you for it; they are always acceptable, and few if any days pass without my remembering to pray for you by name, dear Polly. But now I will tell you a few of the facts of the past week. I finished my last letter on the Saturday night. Before breakfast on the Sunday morning I was called to the dying bed of my dear Lizzie Marks, but I shall want sheets on sheets of paper, and more time than I now have, to tell you of all that took place on that day. Her changed look told me that death was near; and oh, her bright, bright smile of love and thankfulness! I said to her, "Oh, Lizzie, would you not like to go to Jesus on His own Holy Day?" Never shall I forget her expression of almost rebuke when she said, "His will,—I have no will but His will." So earnestly did she entreat her friends to close at once with the present offers of mercy. To her sister she said, "Mary, Mary, I see your red eyes; they are red with weeping for me, but oh! weep for yourself, not for me; I am going to Jesus, and you are trampling on His Blood! Yes, Mary, think of that! you are His murderer! yes, His murderer! You are committing murder every day till you give your heart to Him." And then to her mother, "Oh, come *now!* now is the appointed time, now is the day of salvation." I was singing that verse, "Hallelujah to the Lamb Who died on Calvary!" and she said "Will no one praise God?" Her mother said, "Richard and Mary, do sing;" "No," she said, "they must not sing, they cannot praise God, for they have not given their hearts to Him." Her own bursts of praise were constant, and the last verses of Isaiah xl. were constantly on her lips—"Have ye not heard," etc.; the words "mighty God" she often said. At one I left her just to dine and sit with poor Edwin White, whilst his mother was at John White's funeral; I was away about an hour and a half, and on again going into her room she raised both her arms and exclaimed,

"This is dying, this is dying; Glory be to God!" For an hour she scarcely ceased speaking and praising God; I sang hymn after hymn—"One there is above all others," three times; and never, never shall I forget her burst of joy and praise—"Glory to the Blood; it is all through the Blood! Oh! I see the Sprinkled Blood; it is speaking for me! Oh! I see the Living Bird with the Blood of the Slain Bird on Its wing. I have seen Jesus, and God said 'This is my beloved Son in Whom I am well pleased.' Oh! He is holy, He is pure! pure! pure! pure! and I shall walk with Him in white, for He is worthy and I am worthy and pure in Him; He is my righteousness." She took leave of all, and kissed all, and then said, "He hath given me the kiss of reconciliation." But pen will not do justice to that scene! The last words she addressed to me were, "Hush, hush! I want to hear Him say 'Come up higher.'" Afterwards we heard her say "Goodness—mercy," and without a struggle the happy spirit took its flight. The enemy of souls tempted her almost to the last, but oh! the energy that she would say—"Get thee hence, Satan, I will worship God! Backward shall each foe be driven." I did feel so sorry Mr. Fenton was not there, and I think he was a little annoyed that I did not send for him; but at the last she went more suddenly than I had expected. He had seen her every day for the previous week, and she sent her thanks to him. Oh, he was a blessing and a comfort to her, dear, dear Lizzie! At five minutes after five she entered into rest. I do bless His Holy Name for His saint departed in His faith and fear. I went at once to Leskinnick; indeed it was quite too much to bear alone—Glory be to God. On Monday I was three times at the house; at my morning visit I found the pastor there first, and oh! how sweetly did he pray beside that lovely corpse. In the afternoon, after the class, Miss Powell and I went there together, and put the lovely white camellias in her coffin, and Minnie Gregory printed for me that verse which I also put in the coffin—" When Christ Who is our life shall appear, then shall she also appear with Him in glory." And then at eight in the evening I went to see the poor mother, for they took the body back to St. Just that night, and on Saturday afternoon I drove Mr. Fenton there for her funeral; he gave such a striking address. I do feel my dear Lizzie very much wanting, and so does dear Eliza; but now I must conclude for the present. . . . . .

The Coombe, *October, 1865.*

My dear Miss Haydon,—I was very glad to receive your kind letter this morning, and to get such a comfortable report of your strengthened nerves. With God's blessing on the change of air and scene I do trust after a time that you may be quite able again to resume your important work, and that you may be used and owned by Him unto Whom I am sure you desire to dedicate your time and talents. I am sure the second lesson for to-day must comfort you—S. Luke xii., "The hairs of your head numbered;" The sparrow's fall noticed: lessons of trust from the birds of the air and flowers of the fields.

You may well say "The Bible is a wondrous Book." Aye, He Who knew its contents says, "The Word shall judge you at the last day." Do you remember those lines in Pollock's Course of Time? "They had the Bible;" as if with *that* an open book all who perish will be without excuse; and then he goes on with those lines,

> "Star of Eternity, the only Star that rose on Time:
> Bright candle of the Lord, etc."

By the three p.m. train to-morrow we expect the Fentons. The pastor asked me a week ago for your address in Exeter, as he said he should like to call and see you, but I wrote and told him you were not there.

. . . . We shall indeed be thankful to have our dear pastor back again, and oh! may God bless and keep, and support and strengthen him, and yet use him for His glory. The D——s left on Monday. He I feel did not like me; his sermons were so very good, but to me so utterly wanting in "unction." The congregations kept up, indeed I think he was much liked. The last two Saturdays we have met at Leskinnick, at 11.30; two weeks before at Mrs. Wright's, and once at Mrs. Philippide's, but now she has gone to spend the winter with Mrs. Clutterbuck, and has given up her lodgings. We shall I think be all very glad to find ourselves with you again, dear Miss Haydon. I think your niece returning with you will be a very nice thing. What a pleasant sensible kind-hearted woman is your sister-in-law! I am not surprised at your loving her! God bless you, dear Miss Haydon.

Your very affectionate<br>
E. B. BOLITHO.

*Saturday, 10 a.m.*

My dear Miss Haydon,—I have thought much of you, and should be very thankful to hear your brother was mistaken, and that the longing desire of your heart had been satisfied; but I do wish I had faith for myself as I have for others, and could so realize God's Hand as ordering my life as I can see He does yours. I fear I don't place myself in His keeping with the simple reliance of a child; but I am sure if you do not meet your poor afflicted one, it is because He, Who *is* "Love" and Who does all things well—numbers the hairs of our heads, and marks the sparrow's fall, knows whereof we are made, remembers we are dust, and as a Father pitieth His children—has a wise purpose in the disappointment; He sees you both; His everlasting arms are underneath you both; and He keeps you both as the apple of *His* eye. Don't you remember that sermon of Mr. Lawley's—"All souls are mine?" But I must attend to other things just now; indeed, as there is no London post to-day, I cannot send this till to-morrow.

11 p.m. Before I go to bed I shall chat a little more with you. You will be glad to hear that Mr. Aitken goes on favourably. Dr. Nankivell came from Bournemouth to see him; he hopes if he can get up his prostrated strength that he will do well. I set off to go to Pendeen last evening to make personal enquiries, but the rain prevented my getting so far, though I did get to "Belle Vue" to see the old man Matthews, who still lives. I called on old Mrs. Rogers (Mrs. R——'s mother) this morning; the latter seemed so very pleased at my coming, and the old woman very thankful and quietly happy, enjoying her large print Testament. I missed you and yours at the bible class; Miss Jacobs and Janet Vibert were there. I am reading "Ruth Farnley" aloud to Miss Maynard; it is very pretty. I have been at Gulval three times this week to see such a beautiful dying girl. Yesterday she was quite insensible. I do hope she is a saved soul, but these death-bed conversions are *most* unsatisfactory in general, and this girl is very, very ignorant, having lived without God and not read His Word; it is so difficult to direct to One Who has been "The Unknown God."

My last accounts from Leamington have not been good. Mr. Fenton is weak and incapable of any exertion, almost entirely on the sofa. God's dealings with him are remarkable.

Oh! may we know much of to-morrow's Epistle, and ever rest on the truth that He is Love; and oh! may we draw deeply from that Love. Thank God the Well is deep; oh! may we let down the empty vessel and launch out the net for a draught.

I do hope you may enjoy Mrs. H——'s company; don't overtax your strength, but drink, sleep, and be out as much as possible. And now, with much love and my best wishes, good night.

I remain,
Your very affectionate
E. B. BOLITHO.

Lariggan, *January 3rd.*

My dear Miss Haydon,—I was very glad to hear of your arrival at Crediton, and hope the rest and love you receive there may strengthen and refresh you for the coming struggle of and *for* life. His ways are not ours, but His are equal, though to us they often seem unequal; His *needs be's* are past finding out; "great is the mystery of Godliness," and I am sure great is the mystery of His Providence; but may He give us much faith to rest in the fact that He is our Father and that He pitieth His children. . . . . Please pick up all you can to edify us at the bible class; we did not assemble last week as I had a cold, and Mrs. C—— told me we could not have the room for our "gathering" to-day as the mothers' tea-party was to come off; but now that is postponed as poor Mrs. C—— has gone to lodge at L——, to be near her poor son, who is I hear hopelessly ill of lung disease. I fear he lived too fast, and brought on diseased liver which has most rapidly spread to the chest, and the doctors think a few weeks likely to end his term of existence here. Poor Mrs. C——!

her trials have been great. Bless God, she knows the brother born for adversity and is leaning on the Beloved, and He will bring her through. My throat has been so uncomfortable that I have exposed myself very little to the cold air, though with the help of close cabs have been at all the services, and some of Mr. A——'s sermons have been deeply interesting; and had I your memory could impart many precious thoughts to you, but alas! though, thank God! they leave an unction, I cannot form them into words. Sunday morning was, "We look for light, but behold obscurity;" the evening, "Seest thou this great building? not one stone shall remain on another." It was far-fetched, but thrilling; our building our *own* temple, and *our* call to pull it down stone by stone, and not to let one remain. I went to the late service at eleven; it was very solemn; the church full, and all so very quiet. Mr. A—— preached on "My days are swifter than a post."

It was very encouraging to those who can look to Jesus and not feel their own pulse nor grieve as I do over past failures and present faithlessness; but oh! the Communion was the crowning act of the day. To by faith receive Him as ours alone and bless Him! All-sufficient strength for all the future! "My grace is sufficient for thee." Oh! may we draw more from that inexhaustible store, and venture out in simple and entire dependence on Him Who says "Cast your cares on Me," etc.

We had a very earnest prayer-meeting on Monday, and Mr. A—— preached a deep sermon from Colossians ii., 11, 12, but I was so very sleepy I could not understand it; he means to preach on the subject again; I know you would have liked it.

I am still here, but want to get home on Saturday, but scarcely expect to do so. . . . . .

P

Old Betsy D—— died last Friday; her son and grand-daughter *Betsy Ann* came to me on Saturday, they wanted help to bury her. . . . . . Dear old soul, she was very happy, and is now with the Saviour she loved and long waited for; she was eighty one. . . . . . I hope your sister and her family are tolerable; I am glad Emma is so satisfactory. . . . . . "All souls are Mine;" and He keeps your poor deeply afflicted sister as His purchased blood-bought possession, and it is a safe keeping, and one day together you will praise Him. . . . . . .

And now I will close; this is my third letter, and I am very tired, so with much love and my best wishes,

I remain,

Yours in the love of Jesus,

E. B. BOLITHO.

My dear Miss Haydon,—I am glad you are with your poor sister and can give such a comfortable report of her. One wiser than we said "It is better to go to the house of mourning than of feasting," and I do trust He will give you much of His abiding presence, and

"His presence makes my Paradise,
And where He is is Heaven."

I am glad Mrs. A—— was with her daughter; I conclude she died at Easter. God gives her grace to bear her trial, but still the loss must be terrible, though knowing her dear one is "safe Home" is such a blessed rest for the soul. The weather has not been favorable; to-day it looks *harder*, and I hope we may have a little bright sunshine; for my own feelings it has been hot enough, as to me summer heat is most trying. I did hope to have had my school tea-drinking on Thursday; then, as my brother William's girls did not come back from school till that night, I was asked to put it off till Friday. I had arranged that day, and my brother Tom sent to ask me to put it off, as he wanted to give a tea to all the blind that Mr. Williams teaches, so I must put off mine till the beginning of the week. So far I trust there is no increase of smallpox; I don't fancy there have been more than three cases, and those very mild. You would greatly have enjoyed our sermons on Sunday; both from the Gospel for the day; and plenty of deeper as well as first principle truths did Mr. A—— draw from it. As to the first, the advancing Christian did not *need* the feelings and joy of first love; the finest, sharpest-edged tools were essential for the fine carving, though unsuited for the little child; depths must be fathomed, and often dark and rugged and difficult ones, to get the rich jewels, but only trained ones could venture there. Then such a vivid description of the whole process of fishing: not close to the sandy, pebbly shore, but out into the deep the net was let down, and then not left out hap-hazard, but carefully secured, and the fish even when enclosed were surrounded so that there might be no escaping; that we often, in our efforts to win souls let down the net at random, delivered our souls with a few earnest but often badly-timed words, and then we left it and did *not watch* for the success nor expect the draught. But as usual I fear I may mar, but I know you would have been edified, and by your memory have edified others.

I met in a doorway a few days ago, where we were both sheltering from a shower, a very interesting young woman; she is the St. ——'s school mistress; she gave a clear account of her conversion, and really seemed nice.

I heard from Mary A—— a few days ago, giving the account of the conversion of her second brother; he has returned for a few months to recruit his health, from Ceylon, where he is settled. About a year ago he had a very bad bite from a dog: this impressed him, and then Reed's book, "The Blood of Jesus," plainly showed him and helped him to trust his Saviour.

> "God works in a mysterious way
> His wonders to perform."

I have had the pleasure of seeing Mr. Roe. He drank tea with me last Tuesday before church; he preached that evening from "The whole armour," Ephes. vi. He drank tea here on Thursday with a few others, and spoke so sweetly on the sympathy of the members of Christ with each other. Capt. C—— exemplified this virtue by going with Mr. Roe to the Land's End and staying for a day or two. I fear he will not like it; it is lonely and dreary, and the people very unpleasant and independent; but may the Lord use him there for His glory . . . . . .

The G——'s have given up their sittings at St. Paul's, and gone decidedly to the Brethren. Mr.—— seems to thank God for his deliverance from *their wiles*,[1] and says they nearly drove him to a mad-house. Do beware of playing with edged tools; and now with much love good-bye.

I remain, your affectionate<br>
E. B. BOLITHO.

The Coombe, *Tuesday, 4.20 p.m., June 22nd, 1875.*

My dear Friend,—I have been quite expecting to hear from you; I feel quite anxious to know if you have had the pleasure

---

[1] Plymouth Brethren.

of seeing your poor afflicted sister; if she is well, remember me very kindly to her. I have often thought of you, and missed your Saturday visit. I am glad to hear, but don't trouble yourself to write much; I know when with friends letter-writing is usually accomplished under difficulties, and I wish you to have rest of mind and body, and get all the pleasure you can, and forget that there is a book save One. The subjects at the Mildmay Conference will I am sure greatly interest you; I seem to have no mind to grasp anything.

I hope you found your friends well; don't kill yourself *rushing* about. Fancy the claims of Moody and Sankey before Parliament! More and more do I see what the barley loaf in Gideon's dream (or rather the dream heard) is, being fulfilled. "Not by might nor power, but by My spirit," saith the Lord; and "He will work, and who shall let it." Oh! to be more filled with His spirit that He might hear from us, as touched by Him, "Here am I, send me." I saw Mrs. M—— yesterday; she had been at the Brighton Convention, but though she much enjoyed it I don't fancy had perfect sympathy with all its details. . . . . .

We are to have celebration of Holy Communion at noon on St. John Baptist's Day. Mr. Aitken preached on Sunday from book of Daniel, ix., 10 and 13. You would have liked the evening very lovely sermon on "Standing in our lot," waiting on Him, working, witnessing for Him, looking for Him, but standing in our lot, and that must under all circumstances be the right place and hid in the Cleft Rock, even when He passed by to smite the nations, thus safe in Him. I much enjoyed the Holy Communion, but missed you. To-day the atmosphere is dull and heavy, and I have too much sympathy with it, and am feeling weary and tired; I hope I shall awake up before church time. I saw Mr. T—— this morning; I shall try to go (to his meeting) to-morrow, but of an afternoon I am very weak and dull.

Mr. Aitken was very practical and good at the prayer-meeting yesterday on second morning lesson. Having all things in common he thought most unpractical; the lazy, *good-for-nothing vagabonds* would sit still and let the industrious work for them; but on the teaching of the next chapter, most searching truth in the inward parts,—the being perfectly natural and free from eye-service, the being what we seemed to be. And now goodbye. The Lord be with you and greatly bless you, and restore you ere very long to

Your affectionate
E. B. BOLITHO.

The Coombe, *July, 1873.*

My dear Mr. Savage,—. . . . . . How are you all? And when does the terrible exodus begin? I should like to see the dear sisters before they go, and is it true that dear Mrs. Aitken will leave shortly? I don't like to intrude, as perhaps they may be busy, but let me know their wishes, and when shall I send your two books? . . . . . .

I feel my heart is much with you all. You can have no idea of what the shutting up of that house will be to me; I still often wish to think it is a dream; I feel I cannot settle to anything, . . . . .

Do come to see me if you come to Penzance.

With kind love to you all,
I remain, your affectionate
E. B. BOLITHO.

Is not Doctor Arnold's letter delightful and blessedly true?

The Coombe, *January 19th, 1878.*

My poor dear Mrs. Cay,—Constantly have you been in my thoughts since I learnt a few days ago of the very deep sorrow you are called to bear. The Lord is I am sure a very present help to you, and that you are still knowing that it is the Lord; but oh! how your poor dear warm motherly heart must be bleeding, aye, well-nigh broken. The Son Who had a human mother can alone fully sympathize with you, and He Who remembered her when in the agonies of the cross will not forget you now and poor dear Captain Cay too. Oh, this is a bitter, bitter grief! I see the paper says fever was the cause of your dear one's being taken from you, and at Bombay, on Christmas Eve. Have you had further details? He was the seed of the righteous and the child of so many prayers, and I do trust that you have every reason to believe your dear boy is "safe Home." How you must long to have been near him; I know you very deeply loved your first-born, and could not but feel thankful and proud at his abilities and the progress he had made. I heard him so well spoken of by Cecil Drake, the surgeon of the *Narcissus*, a few days since. All my family feel much sympathy with you and sorrow for your great trial. Arthur spent last Monday with me; he seems a very little boy to be so far from home. I hope the other members of your family are well. With true sympathy for you both,

I remain, dear Mrs. Cay, your affectionate

E. B. BOLITHO.

2, South Parade, *Feast of the Epiphany, 1882.*

My dear Mary (Miss M. E. Tregelles),—I quite believe I sent you and your sister Christmas cards; I know I fully intended to do so, and hope I put the intentions into practice, but really I had so many things to do that I fear some kind friend may have been forgotten. Have you made up your mind on the Christmas card question? I do hope they may be blessed, for God has said His word shall not return void, and so much of His word has been thus circulated and prayed over; but still though small tokens of love they are rather a burden sometimes.

Well, enough of that subject. I do hope you are tolerable again. This very warm weather is in your favor, and if able to get out, you must, I am sure, enjoy the soft air.

My sister always expects me to spend the Christmas season with her; I am very fond of her and hers, but there is so much teaching that I can learn better in the quiet of my own fireside; but I still linger on here; her party is so reduced that they are not willing I should leave them, so home engagements get in arrears.

I trust you have had a happy time, leaning very much on the Beloved and from Him getting much strength and power; none can teach as He does. May the year on which we have entered be one of much blessing; may He use you much for His glory . . . . . .

This is a stupid letter, as mine always are. I mean to enclose one of my bible class cards: I have written on the back of each I have given to my class the text given to me, "Let this mind be in you which was also in Christ Jesus." Will you pray for our little class?

I remain, with kind love,<br>Your affectionate<br>E. B. BOLITHO.

The Coombe, *Saturday, 29th November, 1884.*

My dear Friend (Miss M. E. Tregelles),—I had hoped that ere this you had regained your "frail usual," and am very sorry that Miss Fox did not give me a more improved account. I do so often think of you, and so wish I could sometimes enjoy the pleasure and profit of an hour with you . . . . . . I do find it a little difficult to manage a letter, or you would oftener have that infliction. I look back with pleasure to the visit you allowed me to pay you in October. My niece M. G—— is staying with me; she has just read me the "Life of Mrs. Monsell;" it is a most intensely spiritual high-church book; she is now reading me Ballantyne's last book, "The little Trawler;" I think it is a book that will do good. . . . .

I remain, your affectionate
E. B. BOLITHO.

Falklands, Bournemouth.

Dear Emma (Miss E. Stevens),—I have heard of your dear invalid's increased illness from Mrs. G——, and I expect she has required so much care and attention that you have been too much engaged to allow you time to write to let me hear how she goes on. Remember me kindly to her, and tell her I often think of her, and pray and trust she has peace in her soul. Joy is a fruit, and not our salvation,—it is Jesus, and He alone that saves. His work is done; "It is finished!" Glory be to God! The Father is *perfectly* satisfied, the debt is paid, and we are free. He has paid it, and oh! the mighty Price,—not corruptible silver and gold, but His own precious Blood, and we may venture on That. Oh! let us praise Him for His free love. I will not trouble you with a long letter. I feel much for you and your sister, to whom please remember me; but Jesus will be your Friend if you will both trust Him, and He can never leave nor forsake. May He Himself be very precious to your dear sufferer, make all her bed, and lay underneath His everlasting arms, and at last bring her safe Home and be for ever with Him. Amen. Alleluia.

With true Christian sympathy for you all,

I remain, your sincere friend,

E. B. B.

Lanwithan, Lostwithiel, *August 30th, 1884.*

My dear Emma,—Thank you much for your kind letter; it was forwarded to me here, where I have been since last Monday. I fully intended to be at home this week, but my kind friends here *will* keep me, and provide for me most interesting work, which makes me happy and thankful; but they make far too much of me. *Please pray much for me*, particularly to-morrow afternoon, that I may speak for Him and by His power.

As it will be moonlight next Wednesday, I am going to ask you to help me on that evening. I hope to have the Bible class on that afternoon as usual. I have several to visit this morning, so with much love for your sister and Miss H——,

I remain,

Your affectionate friend,

E. B. BOLITHO.

---

This ends the small collection of friends' letters. Those to her sisters and nieces naturally contain so much family matter, that we have very few suitable or interesting for publication. Of the following, nine are to different relatives, on events specially demanding her sympathy or spiritual help; one is a sweet little Christmas note to a child; and the rest are to her niece, Mrs. Foster, and relate to her frequent visits to Lanwithan, and to the many in whom she was interested there.

## CHAPTER IV.

### *Family Letters.*

(1859—1883).

To a niéce, on spiritual difficulties—To a Goddaughter, on her Confirmation—To Mrs. Foster, on "Sister Dora;" on Rev. W. H. Aitken's Mission at Penzance, 1879; on Birthday; on Moody and Sankey's Mission at Plymouth; New-year's Greetings; Illness of old servant; Meeting Bishop at Pendeen; Easter, 1885—To a sister, on her daughter's death—To Mrs. John Bolitho, on sad anniversaries—To her great-niece, Ruth, for Christmas.

The Coombe, *1859.*

My very dear M——, I was very thankful to get your letter; deeply do I feel interested in you, and I think few, if any, days pass without my praying for you; and I do praise and bless God that He still gives you the hunger and thirst after Him.

I feel your letter is a difficult one to answer, but I commit it to Him, and may He teach me what to say. Dear M——, it is faith in His own Word that you want, and believing it because it is His Word, and therefore it is true, and is for every sinner who will receive it. Look in your Bible at Acts xiii., 38, 39—"Through this Man is preached unto you the *forgiveness* of sins, and *by Him* all who *believe* are *justified from all things:*" then turn to 1 John v., 9—12—God hath given to sinners (as sinners) eternal life; he that *hath* the Son, that is, he who by faith takes Jesus, *has* eternal life, because he has Jesus Who is eternal life; but if we believe not that He is ours, and that He has died for us and made full atonement for all our sins, we *make* God *a liar*, because we don't believe His own record of His Son.

Now this is all easy to write, but I well know difficult to act; but try to cast yourself with all your doubts and all your unbelief on Him, clinging to no *one desire* or *feeling* of your own, but only to His Word.

If Jesus died for sinners, He died for you; and Glory be to God! He did die for sinners; and I know He tasted death for you *because* He tasted death for every man. If I may use the expression, He has no pet sinners to whose romantic, interesting sins He can pander; for, dear M——, *all* have sinned, all have come short of His glory, and all must be saved by taking God at His Word, not by their feelings. I know from my own experience that we hug our doubts, and like to be petted, but God will not have us thus. Look to His Word, and see what that says. You ask, "Can any one be Christ's and not feel sure he is?" That is a difficult question to answer. Rom. viii., 14, 16—"The Spirit beareth witness with our spirit that we are born of God." Now, M——, when we by faith commit ourselves to Jesus, and by faith lay hold of Him—lay all our sins on Him, and leave them on that blessed Sin-bearer, and give our hearts as they are, with all our doubts and fears to Him—the moment we really make this act—not talk about it, not desire it, but launch out and hang on Him alone,—then He at once sends His Holy Spirit to witness with our spirits that we are His

children. Now, dear M——, what do you know of this ?
Mind you, the glimpse of Him may often be clouded, but
still we know we are His children; people so mistake the
gate for the way, and try to walk in the way before they have
really entered into the gate, and so have to go back again
and are very marred. Now, dear M——, we enter the gate
by faith in Jesus alone, but we cannot go in till we have first
given our hearts to Him. Thank God that you do desire to
give your whole heart to Him; the desire all came from Him,
but we may have all the desires and wishes without being
inside the gate; and mind you, He knoweth whereof we are
made, and He remembers that we are dust, but still we must
all come to the point and surrender to Him.

Can you, on your knees and with an honest heart, say, in
the language of the service for the Holy Communion,—" Here
I offer and present unto Thee myself, soul and body, to be a
reasonable sacrifice;" and will you write this down and sign
it with your own name? And sure I am, if by faith and with
an honest (it may be a trembling) heart you do this, that He
will accept it and bless you with the power of His Spirit.
Don't think, "Oh! I can do it to-day, but I shall draw back
to-morrow;" well, do it again to-morrow, do it afresh every
hour, and He will help you; and not let the enemy of your
soul prevail; he may often try and wound you deeply, but
come with the wounds to His Wounds. Glory to God! there
is always healing there; but mind, if we honestly give ourselves to Him we must resolve to go out with Him without
the camp, and bear His reproach; it will be a reproach.
He Himself says, "If any man come after Me, let him
deny himself and take up his cross, and follow Me." I could
write sheets to you, but have not time. Oh! my dear, dear

M——, come out at once, and come out boldly and thankfully; lay hold of Jesus as your Saviour, and *henceforth* let no man trouble you. Give yourself to Him to be His, and *act* and speak "I am the Lord's."

I am very happy and thankful to hear from you, and shall anxiously look for your next letter. Very much love.

Your very affectionate aunt,<br>
E. B. Bolitho.

The Coombe, *June 18th, 1863.*

My very dear ——, As I may not see you alone for some days I shall just write you a little note, to tell you how deeply interested I feel in you, and that I do pray that the solemn service in which you are so soon to take a part may be a real means of grace to your soul.

May you *by*, and *in*, the strength of the Lord be enabled to give your heart *fully* to Him, to Whose service you will to-morrow pledge yourself.

It is a warfare, and a contest, but, dear ——, the glorious loving Captain of our salvation will Himself lead and guide, and by His Holy Spirit *ever* direct those who in *faith* and *obedience* strive by His grace to follow Him. We may and must doubt ourselves, but "Looking unto Jesus" we shall by His power be kept from falling. Venture out of yourself on Him, cling to Him, my dear child; I know you love Him, and still better, He loves you; then trust His love.

May you feel His own loving arms around you to-morrow, and may He indeed seal you His for ever, give you His Holy Spirit to *dwell* in you, and may His blessed fruits be seen in your life.

God bless you; keep the accompanying "Word"[1] as a remembrance of June 19th, 1863. May Jesus indeed be your all in all.

Your very affectionate aunt and Godmother,

E. B. BOLITHO.

The Coombe, *Saturday Night, March 3rd, 1867.*

My dearest Elizabeth,—You may be sure you are much in our thoughts, and most anxious do we all feel for every fresh report of dear ———. I wrote to your mother on Thursday, but that was the day we had such sad reports of your invalid, so I did not like to send it; tell her so, with my kind love. I shall think of her to-morrow. I am so glad you have all had the opportunity of seeing your dear brother; you know how anxious we all are to hear any particulars respecting him. Many, many prayers have, I am sure, been offered for him. I do trust God may give you a word for him. Oh! may he be enabled to see himself as a poor helpless sinner, and Jesus as his precious loving Saviour, Who, as a good Shepherd, has been seeking him; and oh! may the dear one be enabled to lay all his sins on Him Who has borne them in His own body on the tree.

"We are sinners doomed to die,
Jesus paid the penalty."

Oh! dear Elizabeth, how we should love and trust Him. If ——— is well enough to bear it, do give him my very kind love, and tell him, if you think he would like it, how much I think of him, indeed of you all; and oh! may this solemn time be made a great blessing. I have often wished to write to your father, but I felt I could not do it; my heart is very

[1] An illuminated motto, "Jesus."

full when I think of him. What a party you must be. I saw dear Mabel this morning; she is so much more sociable when you are all away. I was in hopes she might have come to me on Thursday, and to The Abbey yesterday: she told me to-day she would come "another evening."

I went to see that poor woman at the Public Buildings this morning. I think I never saw any one so happy; praise is the constant language of her lips, and I believe of her heart.

I saw nurse Trounson too, to-day; she is very unwell. I don't think will ever get better. She told me to-day she should never recover; I do hope God's Spirit is working in her soul: she seems very thankful to be spoken to. A young man of twenty is, I may say, a daily object of interest; he is so anxious about his soul, and I am sure God is seeking him. There is much sickness everywhere. Oh! to be meet for that time when none shall say "I am sick."

I conclude ere this R—— and P—— are with you; I trust the former is better. Miss H—— is very ill,—rather better to-day. Much love to you all.

Your affectionate<br>
E. B. B.

The Coombe, *May 7th, 1870.*

My dearest Elizabeth,—I have seen you so lately I have not much to say; and as I am very tired, and it is past eleven, it is time to prepare for bed; but I must just write you a line, to send you my love and best wishes on your birthday. He is your Peace, and having made peace for you and reconciled God to you, our work is plain,—to *thankfully* receive the peace already made, and *then* we shall, as a proof of having received the peace, ourselves daily endeavour to "follow His blessed footsteps." Just to show I have not quite forgotten you I send you a little book; I know you have such heaps of things that I cannot from my never overfilled purse send you much of a handsome present; but I am so very fond of the little book, that I want you to read it, and I think it will be liked at the Mothers' Meeting. . . . .

The Coombe, *May 7th, 1879*.

My very dear Elizabeth,—I am not going to trouble you with a long letter, but must send you a few words of love and kind thoughts and wishes on your birthday. I do earnestly pray for you, and desire God's best blessings for you. May He fill you with His Spirit, and guide and use you for His glory. I have been struck this week with that expression in the Epistle, 1 Pet., ii.—"That with *well doing* we may put to silence the ignorance of foolish men." I more and more see that it is the consistent Christian life that tells as a power. I so grieve that my influence is so powerless; if I was more occupied with the Lord Jesus Himself it would be so different. If we lived in the sunshine of His Presence we should more reflect His rays, and others would see it and He be glorified. . . . . .

And now, with much love, good-bye.

I remain, dear Elizabeth,<br>Your very affectionate<br>E. B. BOLITHO.

I send second series of "Daniel Quorm." I admire and value the book immensely; the two last chapters are so excellent; it is but a small present, but I know you will accept it and the love that accompanies it.

*The Coombe, August, 1879.*

My dearest Elizabeth,—Mrs. Thomas told me that she had lots to do, so could not stay long; she was looking forward to Mr. W. H. Aitken's service at St. John's Hall, and I conclude was there; every part of the hall was full. I wish you were here. I do feel most thankful he has come; and earnest prayer is offered for a great blessing on the efforts made for the salvation of souls.

I went to St. Mary's on Sunday evening. I had not been there on a Sunday for more than twenty-one years; the church was quite full. I hear they say two thousand people there, and all so attentive. The sermon was sixty-four minutes, and even S—— and B—— did not think it too long. I felt it was a most solemn time to many, perhaps a last message; and to all "the savour of life unto life, or of death unto death." I had expected much, but had far more than I ever expected. The subject was Rev. iii., 20—"I stand at the door and knock." He spoke of the high position the Church of Laodicea had taken, and of all our goodness—Church-going, Prayers, Confirmations, Communions, Schools, Discipline, etc., etc.; but we might be and do all these most desirable and excellent things, and yet not even touch the hem of the Saviour's garments; and unless we had that connecting link, how utterly hopeless and useless was all. Like our looking for fruit from an unplanted tree; it was unconnected with the earth, and so could derive no sap nor nourishment, and so *could not* bring forth fruit. He drew such a vivid picture of the self-satisfied soul—rich, moral, good—*need* of nothing; and until we were sensible of need we could not take food with advantage, it would be of no real service. When we felt the need, Jesus knocked; He came to sup, and always brought the feast with Him;—but I must not go on.

Dear M—— sat very near me; I thought so much of her,—she looked ill, and old and sad. Jesus has knocked at her door! Oh! I want Him so to be the honoured guest in her heart. He comes as a King, and expects the throne. Oh! that we all would lift up the gates of our hearts that the King of Glory might come in.

Last night Willie's subject was, "Seek ye first the kingdom of Heaven." It was so clear and interesting;—but I must go out, for I have lots to do, and it has cleared a little. To-night and to-morrow night there will be addresses at St. John's Hall, at 7.30; and to-morrow at 3.30 he preaches at St. Paul's. A few of us have been meeting daily the last ten days for especial prayer, and it is time to go. W. H. Aitken slept at his brother's, at Paul, last night, and comes back to me to-night. I feel it a great privilege to be allowed to minister to the Lord's dear servant.

Love to R., M., and much to yourself.

From your affectionate
AUNT EMILY.

The Coombe, *Thursday, October, 1879.*

My dear Elizabeth,—You have I know had a trying time, and I am sure you all felt parting with Elsie and her boys. I trust we may in a few days have a telegram to announce their safe arrival at Mentone. I fear she has left it rather late, and this cold east wind will try dear Horton. I am so very, very sorry for her to go. . . . . . . I expect you will have frequent letters, and time does so rapidly pass with those who are as constantly and usefully occupied as yourself. Are you ever going to visit here again?—I don't say "rush." . . . .

I don't think K—— makes the progress I had hoped she might have done; she still often feels giddy, and does not regain her prostrated strength as we might have expected. She cannot walk; I take her for a drive every day...... She is so patient and self-forgetting; I know but few whose character I admire as much as I do hers. I wish I occupied with my "talent" as profitably as she does with hers; and a woman with a warm heart must have more mind and more trust in God than she gets credit for, or she never could have so nobly borne such very deep trials as she has had. A——, too, is so charming, so very bright and cheerful, and never complains of sorrow nor sickness; she is in constant suffering, and the dear little children so very, very delicate. I hope Richard and Mabel are well, and that you are more merciful to the former, and submit to shut windows! I so often think of you all. I shall like to hear of all the people.

I wish your Rector would have a mission; I believe there would be a *direct* work done, if after-meetings and personal enquiries could be made. It seems here that several were impressed when W. Aitken was at Penzance; they have come now to the Methodists, who are holding daily services, saying that no one had helped them, and now they come to the Methodists. Oh! the poor dear Church is so cramped and bound, and souls are passing away, and above all Jesus robbed of His glory, for He *is* glorified in the salvation of souls.

I think I told you I had been much interested in Father Ignatius' preaching at Bournemouth.

Mr. W—— has often been in my mind; I do believe he might be drawn (never driven), and I am sure his life is such a sad, suffering one.

I was interrupted yesterday, and this is my third attempt to-day; and as I want to go into the village I think I must close. How is M. L——? Remember me most kindly to Fräulein. . . . . . ; and now with much love to you all, and many thanks for the happy visit you let me pay you,

I remain,
Your very affectionate
AUNT EMILY.

The Coombe, *New-year's Day, 1880.*

My dearest Elizabeth,—Just a line to send fond love and kind New-year's wishes. I hope to enclose a little card, but am as usual in fearful haste. I think often of you, and know you have very much before you. My Bible class text this year is, "Kept by the power of God." "The Lord Himself is thy Keeper;" may you realize much of His presence.

I have just heard from M. G——; she and S. F—— come here (D.V.) on Friday, to spend a fortnight; M—— will stay on. I had hoped she might not have come till end of month; I feel worn, and should like a month's perfect rest. Oh! how I do feel Mr. Fenton's loss; none knew what a help and comfort even in his invalided state he was.

God bless you all. Thank Fräulein for pretty card. I enclose three half-crowns; I hope Mabel will accept one, and though such a wee offering, I don't like not to send the old New-year's gift to your sisters. I am overwhelmed with work; just returning to St. Paul's.

Your affectionate
AUNT EMILY.

*March 12th, 1880.*

My dearest Elizabeth,— ...... I feel I am "*got*" old, and that in the last year I have been learning the difficult lesson to be willing to be laid aside on the shelf (not easy for me to learn), and I am still most imperfect in it; as, thank God! I can still be out and about, I have fortunately too little time to give way to ennui. I have had a great many sick to visit; one post office clerk is so nice,—he is twenty-two; for ten years in the choir at St. Peter's, Newlyn. He says his Confirmation decided him for Christ.

I am reading Farrar's "Life of St. Paul;" many most interesting touches, but for general reading not as edifying as "The Life of Christ." ..... "Post Haste: a Tale of Her Majesty's Mails," by Ballantyne, is very interesting . . . . "Workmen and Soldiers," by Mrs. Cobbe, is very nice; tells of last French Revolution. . . . . .

Your affectionate
AUNT EMILY.

The Coombe, *Wednesday, 9.30 p.m., 31st March, 1880.*

My dear Elizabeth,—I am thinking much of you, for I am sure it will be a trial for you to part for a time with your dear child; you will both greatly miss her. I know love to her has prompted you to the sacrifice, and I do hope you will have cause to be thankful for the step you have been led to take, and that all may go on well. I know, dear Elizabeth, that like myself, your mind is too anxious; but try, and I am sure you do and will, to give her up to the Lord Who loves her, and Who is ever near at hand, as our Psalm says—"He will fulfil the desire of them who fear Him."

Mr. Drake drank tea here this afternoon. I made the remark that the first sentence of our Creed, if a reality to us, would make everything right; and Mr. D—— gave me such a lift on the subject, by saying, the word "I believe in God" really is "I lean." Is it not lovely? Oh! may we hang more entirely and "lean hard" on Him.

. . . . . . I had a quiet Holy Week, not going to many services, but being much alone in communion. Oh! to enter more and more into the spirit of all the marvellous teaching of the Great Holy Season, and to live in its power. I read "Sister Dora" yesterday; I never heard of such a woman,— strong in mind, body, estate; such a strong will; above all, strong faith and deep love; and what wonders she accomplished. The biography is most fairly written, as her faults are very manifest: do read the book. I wonder if sister Anna has? do ask her. Mr. Twigg, her great friend, is Mr. Lanivit's friend. Mr. Fenton knew Sister Dora, and Maria —— saw her at Bournemouth.

. . . . . . Mr. H—— sent two hundred beautiful cards to the St. Paul's School, for teachers and children. I believe it was a little thank-offering. It is quite a study to look at that man's face; for a long time he has been impressed but did not yield, till about a month since he and his wife realized their sins were forgiven; they were in St. Paul's (London) at the time. On Palm Sunday they received their first Communion. . . . . . .

Much love,<br>
Your affectionate<br>
AUNT EMILY.

The Coombe, St. Luke's Day, 1875.

My dear Elizabeth,—I do feel I have in every way so failed, that post cards are my usual mode of correspondence. I brighten up sometimes, but to sit with eyes closed and in a half sleepy state is what I prefer; and all effort *is* an effort. To day I feel very done: I went to St. John's for early Communion, and have been a little done up ever since;—but I did not mean to inflict my bill of health on you. I think often of you, and am sure you were sorry to leave Windsworth; I should like to have looked in on you there, but I really felt very unfit to visit friends, and I had made no arrangement for my little home work. It is very little I can or do undertake, but I find no one to help me; and though our gatherings are small, and often seem most unimportant, still I am most particular about giving up work. I feel so soon I very likely shall have to give all up, as I am so losing locomotive power.

I very much enjoyed my visit to Plymouth;[1] there was little new to hear or learn as far as man went, but oh! the power of the Lord did seem so very present,—doubts and difficulties seemed to vanish under the truth and perfect sympathy of the Gospel, and it did come with power. All was so perfectly free from energy of the flesh or excitement, all so real and so quiet. I am very glad I went, though I suppose I did more than I should have. I enjoyed very much my little visit to M——, it is such a peaceful home. . . . . .

I was at the Union yesterday; I don't think I ever thought it a more dismal and hopeless place. I came home to a bright cheerful Harvest Tea at St. Paul's; Mr. Martyn was there, and he preached. Many at Church afterwards. E—— and C. B—— had indeed worked hard to decorate it, etc.

[1] For Moody and Sankey's Mission.

I am very sorry that Mr. Hunt, the young man who has accepted the living, cannot leave his present charge till after Christmas; it is so bad for St. Paul's to be left so long with no settled pastor. May the Lord give us patience, and he who is to come much of His grace. . . . . .

Mr. Huxley is to be married to Miss B—— before Christmas; he has been so good and kind to A——. I have been remembering him to-day, "The Doctor's Day—Luke the beloved Physician." I should like to be remembered to the sorrowing family at Ethy; I have thought much of them, and to you they will be a sad loss, and indeed to so many.

. . . . . . I am reading "Father Lowder;" much to interest, but a very great want. That hymn was blessed to a sceptic at Plymouth—

"My only plea Christ died for me,
And take me as I am."

Never shall I forget hearing thousands sing "Nothing but the Blood of Jesus;" and that is so true. Not by any works of righteousness that we ever have, or can do! No, it is Himself! Himself! May we trust Him more, as the hymn says, "Believing and Receiving."

I thought much of Mr. R—— passing through the tunnel last week; I hope he is walking in the Light. I do not like the express train dashing through your station so rudely; I have such a regard and respect for Lostwithiel that it always gives me a pang! I hope Mrs. Thomas is well; remember me to her and Mrs. L—— if returned.

I remain, with very much love,
Your affectionate
AUNT EMILY.

*January 1st, 1883.*

My dear Elizabeth,—I trust your dear mother has had a comfortable night, and that you may see her fairly well. God bless you, my much loved niece. As usual I am in great haste; I hoped to get a little book for you, but found last night that it could not be had, so I can only send a card.

May we daily be anointed with the fresh oil of the Holy Spirit. Your affectionate
AUNT EMILY.

The Coombe, *Monday Night, 1883.*

My dear Elizabeth,—It was indeed but a passing look I had of you on Thursday! I think it less and less possible to see one's friends, but I don't love you the less, dear Elizabeth, and I remember you daily before One Who can really help, and is so near at hand to you.

Be sure to remember me most kindly to James Freethy;[1] I think he will get better, but blessed to know that he can rest his soul on the Saviour Whom he has long known and loved. . . . . .

I enclose a little book if J. Freethy is well enough to accept it. . . . . .

The Coombe, *Wednesday Night, December 5th, 1883.*

My dearest Elizabeth,—An invitation to spend a few days with you is a tempting bait, but much as I should like to do so, I think for many reasons I must refuse, thanking you very much for your wish to see me. I really do not feel well enough to leave home; lameness increases, and at present I think myself very unfit to leave home. Jane Moyle is staying with

---

[1] An old family servant—an earnestly religious man—who had been ill, and whom she had visited while staying with Mrs. Foster.

me, and will I hope remain till end of next week; she is such a kind help. Then I daily go to 3, Clarence place, to see the poor Tyackes; and as each day we almost expect E―― must pass away, I should not like to leave poor Mary and her sorrowing sister. Then I am very anxious about several cases of typhoid fever; I don't go into their houses, but I can get little comforts for them. So I shall not inflict any more reasons on you. I should like to meet, and hear Mr. Carter preach very much, but I am getting to be very independent of means; I have for the last two months been able so very seldom to get to church. I want stirring up and teaching very much, for I feel low, and nervous. . . . . . With very kind love to you all, I remain, dear E.,

Your affectionate aunt,
E. B. BOLITHO.

I hope Mrs. Pearce will get helped; remember me to her; I shall not forget her.

The Coombe, *May 7th, 1884.*

My dearest Elizabeth,—I am very incapable of doing anything, but I can still and do love you very much, and wish this letter to convey to you once more this assurance, and a large slice of it for your birthday, and every kind thought and wish to accompany it. My little offering is not all I could wish, but I shall be pleased if you will accept it, and find some place for it. I did so wish to write to Mabel, but I was in bed at Clifton that day; but I did not forget her, and trust that God will bless and use her for His glory. Richard is, I hope, "himself again," and able to undertake his work. At present I am quite laid aside, and am not very sanguine as to the future, but I must leave it all. I never felt so perfectly helpless—"Without one thought to plead that's good;" but the Lord is our Strength, and His grace is sufficient for every hour of need. I hope you may have a holy, helpful, happy time at Truro next week; I should like to join you, and shall not forget you.

I was sorry to give you that rude rapid go-by in the express on Saturday evening. I have a bad cough and foot, so am quite confined in-doors.

With kind love, I remain, dear Elizabeth,

Your affectionate

AUNT EMILY.

The Coombe, *July 30th, 1884.*

My dear Elizabeth,—Just a few words to thank you for your kind letters. You are at home again, and I fear as busy as ever. The Gospel for this week tells us about the gathering up of fragments. I do so increasingly feel that there is no health in me; and oh! how much left undone that might and should have been done; and now it seems so difficult to gather up even fragments. Thank God! we are saved by Him and His work alone; but oh! how sorry one feels at the little progress made, the little fruit borne;—but I am not going to trouble you with my poor experience. I do hope we may soon have the pleasure of *looking* on you at Trengwainton.

I very much enjoyed last week, and found the Bishop's[1] most spiritual and practical addresses very edifying, and do trust that the good seed the Master gave to him to sow may bring forth much fruit for His glory.

I was at the Confirmations at Gulval, St. Mary's, and Pendeen. At the last place I had the great pleasure of some personal

[1] G. H. Wilkinson, Bishop of Truro, 1883.

interviews. Mr. Meeres was so very kind, and placed me next the Bishop at tea, and asked me to take him into the church, where I am sure he remained quite ten minutes in rapt contemplation and prayer at the head of the beautiful brass that covers the tomb of my beloved friend Mr. Aitken. The Bishop spoke so kindly and simply to about one hundred church members who had tea in the garden, and explained to them the designs on the Pastoral Staff. K—— and C. B—— were there, and they were so delighted. The Bishop wished for prayer, and Mr. and Mrs. Meeres, Mr. Roe, and myself went into the study, and there he prayed so sweetly, and gave us all his blessing. He was so kind and good, and humble; I never expected to have had such a pleasure. He is the fifth Bishop I have met at Pendeen, but I suppose I shall not be likely to be there again. I am getting very old, and the Meereses are leaving for Perran soon.

Your father kindly asked me to Trengwainton, but there were several others there who from position and intelligence had far greater claims for his attention. I hope you have enjoyed him this week. Mr. Hunt is gone to Samaden as chaplain for August, and Mr. F—— is to take his duty here. Mr. Townend took the service last night; it was a nice sermon. Mr. Hunt had about twenty-six well-prepared candidates, and on Sunday eighty-nine communicants.

I am so glad your mother and E—— have been able to go to church. C—— has a lovely day for the Sunday School treat at Trengwainton. Your father is just going to lunch with me; so with much love for you all,

I remain, dear Elizabeth,
Your very affectionate
AUNT EMILY.

> The Coombe, *September 3rd, 1884.*

My dear Elizabeth,—I will not *burden* you with an extra claim on your time by a long letter, but must just send a line to tell you how much I valued my visit to Lanwithan, and appreciated all your endless kindnesses; accept love and many thanks. I could wish you had more rest and fewer interruptions. I had a very quiet journey home,—I needed it; and do find the truth of that verse—"They who wait on the Lord shall renew their strength.". . . . . .

> The Coombe, *Easter Eve, 1885.*

My dearest Elizabeth,—Much love, and every kind wish for you all at this Holy Season. May Our Risen Lord be increasingly precious, and may we, knowing Him as Our true Paschal Lamb, keep the Feast with joy. I hope to see you very soon.

I wish you would bring your Kingsley's poems with you, that your mother may read "Saint Maura." In real haste,

Your loving
AUNT EMILY.

> The Coombe, *August 22nd, 1883.*

My dearest Sister,—I don't know how to write. Oh! my heart does indeed go out to you all. I am quite sure that you can and do praise God that your precious child has entered into rest,—the struggle over, the victory gained. The Captain of our salvation perfected through suffering, and He has led His dear child

> "Through no darker room
> Than He went through before."

Oh! to know your darling was to love her. But I must not pour out my heart thus. You have all been so brave; the Lord your Keeper, and He will keep. I should much like to see her laid in her last earthly resting-place, but expect you would not wish it; do use me as, and when, you can. For more than seven years you and yours have been the grand object of my life; the smallest incident in yours has been a matter of interest, deep interest to me. I look forward for more particulars; do write as often as you can.

I have been to-day faintly picturing her look of wonder and delight, remembering no more the anguish; for ever with the Lord.

I long to look on you all. Kiss those precious children. Oh! so much more love than I can express for you all, from

Your loving sister,
E. B. BOLITHO.

The Coombe, *August 20th, 1880.*

My dear Elsie,—I should like to see you, and tell you I do not forget you to-day,[1] indeed, remember you every day. I send you verse 25, Jer. xxxi. I thought it so suitable for you when I read it this morning,—the weary satiated, the sorrowful replenished.

Much love, your affectionate
AUNT EMILY.

I am reading Lady Hope's last book; some nice thoughts.

The Coombe, *Saturday, August 19th, 1882.*

My dear Elsie,—Just a few lines to tell you I don't forget you. He Who has been your help will be your hope and

[1] Anniversary of husband's death.

strength unto the end: He allows you to work for Him; for you, He is so full of teaching; and truly in seeking to help others we get helped. I send you much love. What a lovely chapter is our second lesson, Romans xvi.; and a greater than St. Paul tells us in St. Matthew xxv. what He thinks of His helpers. I feel as if I was almost out of that pale, my life seems so indirect and lukewarm. Oh! that all would have the blessedness of working while it is day! I feel the night so fast coming. . . . . .

*The Coombe, Monday, 10 a.m., May, 1884.*

My poor dear Elsie,—I know you love me too much to believe I would intrude on your sacred grief, but I feel I must just send you a line of sympathy which I truly feel for you in this very great sorrow.[1] I do feel so shocked, for though I as yet know no particulars, still I hear the sad event was most sudden. I am so glad you were there, though I fear its effects for you when the re-action comes; but His Word is true—"I am with you always," and He in Whom you trust will be your *present* help in this time of trouble. I did not mean to write as much. With true Christian love

I remain, your affectionate

AUNT EMILY.

I so often remember you and your sad household.

The Coombe, *Monday Morning, October 6th, 1884.*

My poor dear Elsie,—I will not intrude a letter on you, but feel as if I must just write a line to tell you how often I think of you, and how very, very sorry I am at your fresh

[1] Mother's death.

sorrow.[1] May the Lord Himself be your Comforter and Present Help in this time of deep trouble; and He says, "Be still, and know that I am God."

With kind regards and sympathy to your sorrowing party,

I remain, dearest E.,
Your truly sympathizing
AUNT EMILY.

The Coombe, *Saturday, July 18th, 1885.*

My dear Elsie,—You have, I know, been hurrying about most of the week, but I fancy your Sunday engagements may be attraction enough to cause you to settle down at home for to-morrow, so I write, under much difficulty, a line of love to wish you much blessing and His joy and peace on your birthday. I trust God may long continue your valuable, useful life. He has been with you in the midst of your deep trials, and "Christ leads us through no darker room than He went through before."

Have you a photo of the Bishop? I do so want to be allowed to give you one; will you let me know this?

The carriage has come, and I cannot write more, but with much love and every kind wish,

I remain,
Your very affectionate
AUNT EMILY.

The Coombe, 7 *p.m., Wednesday, St. Michael's Day, 1885.*

My dear Elsie,—. . . . . I enjoyed the service this morning: prompt, willing obedience; His glory their delight, and therefore on His will and service they wait. How the *seen*, the

---
1 Sister's death.

actual *un*reality makes the *reality* the "unseen" take the wrong place! Had the disciples been watching they might have ministered to their Lord in agony, but they lost that opportunity. I liked Mr. R——'s sermon very much, but it was most inferior to Mr. A——'s last night, which you would have greatly enjoyed.

I hope to come to you to-morrow. . . . . . Of course you have read Keble's hymn for to-day? One line in it I think the most beautiful in the "Christian Year." . . . . .

Your affectionate<br>AUNT EMILY.

The Coombe, *December 22nd, 1883.*

My sweet little Ruth,—I hunger to see you, and quite long to have you, and next summer we hope for that pleasure. Ann and I talk about you every day, and wish we could hear your dear little voice. Mrs. Uren is very well, and so is "Janie,"[1] who is often a thief. Christopher would, I am sure, be pleased to drive you out again.

Next Friday Horton and Evelyn have a Christmas Tree, and we are asked to come, and we shall all have a present.

I hope you will have a happy Christmas; I pray for you and dear Robin every day. Ann's very kind love; I am going to give her at Christmas your and dear Robin's pictures. I sent to Torquay for them; she does not know, but she will be so glad. I send you a card and a little book, and a shilling, and please give your cousins the cards marked for them. I am sure you love the dear baby.

Much love, and dozens of kisses to you, from

AUNT EMILY.

[1] The cat.

## CHAPTER V.

### *Reminiscences.*

Letters from friends:—Preb. Hedgeland, Rev. R. W. Aitken, Rev. W. Hay Aitken, Rev. R. J. Martyn, Rev. R. J. Roe, Miss M. Tyacke, Miss J. Moyle, Miss Haydon, Mrs. Cay, Miss M. Tregelles, Miss Anna Maria Fox, Sister Anna, Mrs. Herbert, Rev. A. L. Palmes—Extracts from Diary—Visits to Lanwithan—To Trevaylor to meet the Bishop—Last Letter—Illness—Death.

Her letters speak for themselves; further evidence is scarcely needed to show the great purpose of Emily Bolitho's life, but from the humility and self-mistrust with which she wrote, they would give no adequate idea of the wide extent of her influence, or the wonderful success that crowned her efforts, without the following testimony gratefully borne by those who knew her best; and it is striking how from very different points of view, and in varying modes of expression, all give a remarkably similar definition of her character.

In order, however, to explain a little the circumstances under which her work was carried on, we must revert for a moment once more to the time of her introduction to Mr. Aitken, in 1854.[1] From that day forward she appeared fully to realize both what God had done for her and what He would have her do, and to devote herself body and soul to His service.

1 See page 19.

The next few succeeding years were times of great Church revival, and at Penzance its chief development was in the recently erected Church of St. Paul's.[1] Many stirring preachers occupied its pulpit,[2] and at various times assisted in its evangelizing work. Into all the varied details of this work—Bible classes, Prayer-meetings, Mission services, etc., Emily Bolitho threw herself with her wonted energy, laboring loyally with each of the many different Incumbents of St. Paul's; nor can we, in these days of women's advancement in all public work, both religious and secular, imagine what a sensation her zealous activity caused thirty or forty years ago. Such labors as hers were then unheard of, and raised such strong opposition and unpopularity that it required all her earnest faith in, and love for, her Lord, to enable her to overcome them, and to persevere as she did, without flinching.

After her father's death she identified herself completely with the church and parish of St. Paul's, but during his life-time they both attended regularly their parish church of Madron, where Prebendary Hedgeland, now Vicar of St. Mary's, was then Curate. He says:—

"I first made 'Aunt Emily's' acquaintance in 1854, when I became Curate of Madron. At that time she always accompanied her father to morning service at Madron church, and when the Sacrament was administered I always brought the Elements to him in his seat.

"I think the first saying of hers which I remember was to this effect—'You know I always take people on their own assumption, and if any one claims to be a converted person, I always talk to him as being such.'

---

1 Built by Rev. Henry Batten.
2 Among others Rev. W. Haslam, Rev. G. Savage, Rev. R. W. Aitken, Rev. G. Fenton, Rev. R. J. Roe, Rev. T. L. Williams.

"When I came to Penzance, in 1860, I soon found out what an intimate and extensive knowledge she had of the poor and suffering. One woman to whom she introduced me, was held in great veneration by a large circle of people. She had been a bed-lier for years; and her bed was a sort of pulpit to which people resorted to hear words of wisdom and counsel. There was indeed a perceptible atmosphere of holiness in her presence; and when I administered the last Sacrament to her, the room was full of a sympathising congregation. But Aunt Emily, while she loved Catherine Crossman, more than once said to me: 'You know she is a thorough Wesleyan,' meaning that there were elements of narrowness in her which detracted from the completeness of her spiritual character.

"Aunt Emily herself was very broad in her sympathies, and recognised and felt herself akin to goodness wherever it was to be found. Her great friend and adviser was Mr. Aitken, of Pendeen, and no one ever took his place with her. She gave up her time to the sick, the afflicted, the aged; she delighted in young people. I found traces of her presence continually as I was visiting. She was a frequent sharer in the sick Communions of my parish. She was very fond of our Saints' Day Celebrations at St. Mary's, and hardly ever missed one. She often told how much she enjoyed the quiet of those services. She used to look upon Easter Eve as *my* day: I had early (and somewhat often) preached on it, and had told her, that to me it was the most congenial day of the year.

"After her death I was told that she had expressed her hope that, when the time came, she might receive her last Sacrament at my hands. I did not know of this; but it so happened, in the providence of God, that her last Communion was in St. Mary's church, on one of the Saints' Days about

Christmas, 1885; I think it was St. Thomas's Day. That was the last time of her going to church.

"She was a large-hearted woman,—shrank from pain, and was persuaded that she could not bear pain patiently. But I think she did.

"It was a privilege to have known her."

---

The Rev. R. W. Aitken, Vicar of Paul, eldest son of Emily Bolitho's old friend at Pendeen, was Incumbent of St. Paul's from 1869 to 1877. He writes:—

"I wish I could furnish you with letters from Miss Bolitho to enlarge your selection from her correspondence, but the few which I received from her were either on such passing incidents as did not suggest preserving them, or else on ministerial subjects, and therefore unavailable for publication. You are aware, however, that she was so constantly my friendly counsellor whilst I held the living of St. Paul's, Penzance, that I am sure you will allow me to add a little to your collection of memoirs.

"Perhaps a short summary of what one concluded about Miss Bolitho, on reviewing the period of our acquaintance, may be the best aid I can offer in your work.

"As soon as Miss Bolitho had fully realized that God had called her to a distinct line of work in her life, she seems to have bravely set her purpose honestly to do that work, however difficult and often disheartening to herself it might appear to be; she felt that she was placed by God in a position to influence others for good, not only amongst her humble friends of her well-known and much-valued Bible class, and of her district, but also in that social circle in which she herself was called to move in daily life. One can hardly estimate the importance of a life devoted to such a purpose. Instead of the prohibitive stiffness of manner and conversation too often adopted by religious devotees, Miss Bolitho possessed such a lively, hearty, and good-humoured style, and brilliant and piquant flow of conversational power, coupled with such eminent *tact*, that she won her way to hearts of the young *especially*, and to win them to herself was, with her, the step to win them to God; in fact, she carried God with her into the world-life, and men and women acknowledged the influence which such a life gave her. One thinks, with great satisfaction, of those many in her own social position who still cherish the sacred influence which Miss Bolitho's life and words were the means of stirring into vigorous life. As to that part of our acquaintance which pertains to ministerial communication, one feels almost thankful to have to testify that her experience was different from what many supposed. Outwardly bright and cheerful, few indeed knew through what troubled waters God safely piloted her course of spiritual life. Her almost over-sensitive conscience often clouded for awhile her brighter experience, and as her well-known sympathy caused her to be the depository of the secret doubts and fears (on both ecclesiastical and more strictly spiritual questions) of her large circle of acquaintances, naturally enough this re-acted on her own mind, and although her allegiance to her Church and to her God were never really in danger, yet she had periods of severe trial of her faith. Then, like all who are naturally of a lively disposition, she had times of great depression of spirits; yet at the call of duty this was nobly overcome for the sake of others. In the Church, her loyalty to the various ministers who occupied St. Paul's was undeviating; she might not agree with all that was said or done, but she recognised the office rather than the officer, and was not only loyal herself but helped greatly to keep together in unity a peculiar congregation.

"Of outward religious duties I need say nothing, every one saw for themselves what her rule of life was. *Possibility* was the standard of her attendance on means of grace. If St. Paul's was open, she was there; if not, she might be found elsewhere. As to her influence in her own neighbourhood and family, probably you have abundant other sources of information.

"To sum up this short remembrance, she had in this world the reward of a life devoted to others, the reward of a life of love. The children loved her, for she loved them; the young people loved her, for in her they found sympathy in all their little troubles and cares of every kind; the poor, the sick, and the aged loved her, for both heart and purse were open to them; and the Church loved her, for she helped to bear the burden of others, and thus 'fulfilled the law of Christ.'"

---

The Rev. W. Hay Aitken, the Mission Preacher, younger son of Mr. Robert Aitken, of Pendeen, confirms his brother's testimony in many points:—

"It always seemed to me that the great lesson of Miss Bolitho's life lay in her determination to forget herself, in order to promote the glory of God, and the good of her fellow creatures. No one who only knew her slightly, and formed their judgment of her from her bright and ever beaming face, and her happy cheerful manner, would ever have dreamt that she was the sort of person to be attacked by morbid doubts and misgivings as to her own relations with God; yet I believe it would have been easy for her to become a confirmed 'religious valetudinarian, or even a hypochondriac,' if she had not had the wisdom resolutely to look away from herself and her phases of experience, and as I have said, to forget herself in the service of God and man. Hence, although she would sometimes tell her more intimate friends that she did not 'feel' what she heard other people describe of spiritual joy and ecstasy, yet I am persuaded she actually led a very happy life, because she was content to walk by faith, and to 'do the next thing' without distressing or weakening herself by habits of morbid introspection. But, if she did not allow what she considered to be the defects in her experience to depress her, they affected her in another way, for no doubt they contributed to induce in her a very remarkable humility; she was certainly one who exemplified the Apostolic maxim in thinking any one and every one better than herself. Although her faithful and devoted life was a standing sermon to all who knew her, she never seemed possessed of that self-consciousness of superior sanctity which not unfrequently gives, at any rate, a flavour of spiritual pride to the character of otherwise excellent people. She 'wist not that the skin of *her* countenance shone,' but it did shine none the less, others could see how brightly.

"Perhaps the feature in her character that most impresses one's memory, was her perfect naturalness. It is a comparatively rare thing, I am afraid, to meet with a thoroughly spiritual and devoted person who is wholly free from sanctimoniousness, but Emily Bolitho seemed to have none in her composition; she did not lack reverence, but she could not be unctuous, and I believe this was one great secret of the extraordinary influence that she exercised over all who knew her well. She could be very faithful, and say very strong things in a very straightforward way; but there was so much of kindness in her, that it was difficult not to take her candour in good part. She never forgot old friends, and although her circle of friendship was a very wide one, its extension did not seem to weaken the intensity of her attachment to those who were admitted into it. Her memory is very precious to me, as of one of the truest and sincerest friends I ever had; and it is still difficult to realize that her genial smile and kindly face are never again to welcome me in any flying visit I may pay to dear old scenes in the far west. I am only one of many who miss her sorely still. But the light lingers when the orb has set, and the lesson of her life is powerful to-day, like the fragrance of Mary's ointment; it seems to say,—forget yourself; live for God and live for man, and leave it to God to remember you."

---

The Rev. R. J. Martyn, Rector of Buryan, who succeeded the Rev. R. W. Aitken as Incumbent of St. Paul's, says:—

"During the few years of my incumbency of St. Paul's, Penzance, from 1878 to 1882, I had naturally many opportunities of communion with Miss Emily Bolitho, both in our common church life, and also in the friendship which she kindly shewed to me and my family.

"In the one, while her faith gave her joy in the fact that 'for freedom did Christ set us free,' her apprehension of 'the faith' was made with so large a heart, that she was able to look beyond the formula by which truth is expressed, to the truth itself; and to her, religion was that of life rather than of opinion.

"In the other, she was frank, true, cheerful, humorous." . . . .

---

Another clergyman once connected with St. Paul's was the Rev. R. J. Roe, Rector of Lanteglos-by-Camelford. He writes :—

. . . . . . "You have asked me to give you my impressions of the late Miss Emily Bolitho. What always struck me about her, was her intense love and concern for those around her. The wonderful gathering up of all she loved and knew, in prayer; her quick forgiveness of a slight; her natural separation from the world, without 'Stand by, I am holier than thou;' her being 'In the world, and yet not of it;' her complete freedom from cant; her great naturalness, geniality, vivacity, liveliness; marvellous hospitality without display; laying herself out for her friends; keen sense of the ridiculous; great descriptive power and word painting. The world certainly was the poorer when her spirit left it!"[1]

---

From the testimony of her clerical friends we turn to that of a few of her most intimate companions of her own sex. Of these, the principal one, after the girlish friendships of her early days already mentioned, was Miss Mary Tyacke, of Nansloe, Helston, who, until her coming with her sisters to

[1] The *present* Vicar of St. Paul's—Rev. J. J. Hunt, kindly sends, as his contribution, his funeral sermon, which will be found in its natural place at the end of the volume.

live at Penzance, often spent weeks and even months alone with Emily Bolitho, at the Coombe; her sympathetic co-operation is constantly referred to in the letters. She says:—

"It is not easy to write for others a few recollections of a very dear friend whose love and sympathy were never failing for nearly forty years. Those who knew her slightly can remember her bright face, her never-failing stock of amusing anecdotes, and also how with it all she was always ready to speak a word for her Master whenever there was an opportunity; but as a faithful, sympathizing friend, her loss can never be supplied to those who knew her intimately.

"From the time of her visit to Pendeen, in 1854, though every now and then harassed by doubts and fears, she clung to her Saviour, and was enabled to bear witness everywhere to His faithfulness and truth, using every opportunity of doing good to the souls of those with whom she came in contact.

"Just two or three cases will show how faithful she was, and may encourage others to 'follow in her train.'

"One member of her Bible class told me that Miss Bolitho spoke to her about her soul, at one of Mr. Fenton's prayer-meetings. She did not like it at first, and avoided Miss Bolitho, but the latter never missed an opportunity of speaking faithfully to her whenever she met her. After a long time —— saw she had been resisting the Holy Spirit all the time, and became so unhappy she could not rest without opening her mind to her kind friend. She went the same night to the Coombe, and told Miss Bolitho the burden of sin was more than she could bear. Miss Bolitho told her that God had laid it all on Jesus more than 1800 years ago, and begged her to accept Him as her Saviour, and to praise God for His 'at love in providing such a salvation for her. Through

His mercy she was enabled to do so, and she left the Coombe that night rejoicing in her Saviour. She is still living,—a quiet, consistent Christian woman, anxious to work for the Lord; and she often blesses Him for sending such a faithful friend to point her to Him for salvation.

"Once, during her father's life-time, when confined to her room with a bad cold, a young friend staying in the house came to enquire for Miss Bolitho. She was reading her Bible and did not wish to be interrupted, but thought as her friend had come in she would have a little conversation with her, in the course of which she spoke of the danger of living in an undecided state,—half for God and half for the world, and told her friend that if unconverted people could thank God for nothing else, they were bound to praise Him that they were not then lost eternally, &c. Her young friend did not make any reply *then*, but the next morning she came in again, and said—'You were not confined to your room for *nothing* yesterday; when I left you God showed me I was undone—under condemnation; I threw myself on my knees and thanked Him that I was out of hell, because I felt I deserved to be there, and He has shown me that Jesus is the Saviour of the lost—*my* Saviour, and that His precious Blood has washed away all my sins.

"Many similar instances might be related amongst strangers and people of different classes in the neighbourhood and elsewhere, but these will be sufficient to show how God blesses a faithful word spoken in season by one whose daily prayer was—

> 'O strengthen me, that while I stand
> Firm on the rock and strong in Thee,
> I may stretch out a loving hand
> To wrestlers with the troubled sea.'

"The same love for souls continued to the very last. Only a fortnight before her death she wrote to me as follows, from a relation's house where she was staying:—

"'Trevaylor, Penzance, *Tuesday, 11 a.m., December 8th, 1885.*

"'Dearest Polly,—I hope some day to have a quiet talk with you over the experiences of the past week. I hope and believe the dear Bishop has done me good, but how I do wish he expressed himself more clearly on first principles—1 John, i., 2, is a better teacher. I am sure the Bishop knows it all for his dear self, and I thank God for such as he. I should like to be at St. Paul's this evening, but cannot manage it, and so prepare for a quiet evening with E——, who is so charming. I have felt better for the entire change of air and life, except my eye has been very painful, and to-day I don't intend to go out, nor do I intend having the Bible class to-morrow afternoon. Will you tell Miss Vibert this? I think I have told the others I mean to come home on Friday.

"'I find everywhere, if one grasps it, there are opportunities of speaking a word for The Master. I feel there is much that should be done before Christmas, and as yet don't know how it can be done, but I mean to try more to trust Him, and do the next thing.[1]

"'I conclude you go to Helston at Christmas. I am glad your niece is with you; remember me to her.

"'With love to auntie, I remain,
"'Your loving
"'E. B. BOLITHO.'

[1] It seems a remarkable answer to this special effort of faith that her life and strength were spared just long enough for her to complete all her Christmas work.

"She felt fearful sometimes that those she was interested in might be deceiving themselves, and saying 'Peace, peace,' where there was no peace. 'Does she feel herself a leper in the sight of God?' she would ask; and when told once that a person she had great reason herself for doubting had 'found peace,' she characteristically exclaimed 'My dear, she has never found *war* yet!'

"Another trait was her very liberal Christian spirit; she could not bear to hear any unkind things said about others, however she may have differed from their opinions, and she always thanked God for any good she saw in them.

"Her conscience was very tender, and if betrayed into any sudden quickness of temper her sorrow was very great, and she would not only ask God's forgiveness, but also that of those to whom she had spoken. Another fruit of the Spirit in her was the forgiveness of injuries; she seemed unable to retain a feeling of resentment against any one, and when treated unkindly or spoken evil of, she would take the earliest opportunity of showing some real kindness to prove her forgiveness.

"She always read the daily Psalms and Lessons as long as her sight lasted, and would pause and turn each verse that struck her into prayer or praise as she read it; and in speaking or writing to friends during the day would often refer to a subject that was in the Church's daily course of reading. All the services in the Prayer Book were very precious to her. She valued very much the teaching in the Collects, Epistles, and Gospels for Sundays and Holy Days, and always spoke of the lessons to be learnt from them at her Bible classes.

"Hymns,[1] too, were a perpetual source of comfort to her;

---

[1] "Lyra Germanica," "The Christian Year," and "Dr. Monsell's Spiritual Songs," were special favorites.

she liked to have them repeated in the carriage when we were out together, and at many other quiet times. One in 'Lyra Germanica,' for the Eighth Sunday after Trinity, she was never weary of hearing, especially this verse—

> 'O Fount ! O Spirit ! Who did'st take and show
> Things of the Son to us ; Who crystal clear,
> From God's throne and the Lamb's, dost ceaseless flow
> Into the quiet hearts that wait Thee here ;
> I open wide my mouth, and thirsting sink
> Beside Thy Stream, Its living waves to drink.' "

---

Another friend of long standing, Miss Jane Moyle, of Helston, in answer to a request for letters, says :—

"What would I not give to possess even *one* only of our dear Emily's almost weekly letters for years past, but I am grieved to say I can only look on her writing in books she used so kindly give me at my birthdays and Christmas-tides. Oh! had there ever been an idea I should be spared to outlive her, how those letters, so valued and fragrant with the name of Jesus, should still have been among my few earthly treasures. Thirty-three years of correspondence (extracts from) would indeed be priceless! for I may venture to say they were always full of love and praise, and, like yourself, I quite think their being handed down to the younger generation might be blessed.

"Her chief characteristic was always thinking for others, and how she could benefit them both spiritually and bodily; consequently she was bright and happy, full of anecdote, with the most retentive memory combined with love of truth, which gave such a charm and freshness to her conversation. Well I remember dining with her at Mr. B——'s (it must be nearly forty years since); dear Emily left us to go to some evening service at St.

Mary's. I am sorry to have forgotten who the clergyman was, but she was greatly struck with his sermon, and in our presence stood up in the room repeating aloud all he had said, with such earnestness in her looks and tone as greatly to surprise me then, and draw forth my admiration; but how I loved her years afterwards! when she was indeed a most faithful friend to whom I confided everything. Daily do I miss her, and trust one day to be re-united.

"How free from murmuring was her loss of sight, or failing sight, and as hour after hour I used to read the Bible aloud with good books to her, she did not weary but seemed to drink it in with such delight; truly was she a woman of prayer, for however weary and tired the body might be, she was at all times ready for *that*, and refreshed at once."

---

Another lady who enjoyed constant intercourse with her, and to whom Emily Bolitho was a means of much help and blessing, was Miss Haydon, of St. Mary's College for Girls, Penzance. She has kindly given us several of her friend's letters, and adds :—

"You ask me for some recollections of dear Miss Bolitho; they are so numerous that I scarcely know where to begin, in fact she is so connected with Penzance, that, when she left us for her Home above, it seemed literally to me as if 'all joy were darkened, the mirth of the land had ceased.' My heart seemed knit to hers like the soul of Jonathan to David. I had known her for ten or twelve years as an acquaintance, but from my meeting with her at York House, where Rev. R. Aitken, of Pendeen, gave lectures, we became friends indeed, and thank God for the help He sent me through her. The Lesson for her birthday used to be 'the man bearing the pitcher of water'—Mark xiv., 13. Ah! how often has she been the means of lifting that water to my lips. I cannot tell you what her sympathy meant, unless placed as I was, far from my own family and having the battle of life to fight alone; she was so human, and reflected so much of His love 'Who is *touched* with the feeling of our infirmities.'

"During twenty years I attended her Bible class—and what a bond it was!

"One of her favorite passages when things seemed dark and mysterious, was—'What I do thou knowest not now, but thou shalt know hereafter.'. . . . . .

"Miss Bolitho had a great deal of humour, and could enjoy a joke as much as any one.

"She truly ministered 'the Spirit' in the sense in which St. Paul used the term; no fear prevented Miss Bolitho from telling the truth, and yet it was done with such humility that no one could take offence. My last Bible class (I have the passage marked) was on St. Andrew's Day, and the part dwelt on was 'Come and see.' 'Experience—this is the best proof. Andrew did not go into *proofs* that Jesus was the Messiah (though he might have done so), but it was—Come, I have found for myself, now you come and do the same. How difficult it is to speak to one's own, yet Andrew goes to his brother; how consistent must his conduct have been to have given him courage to do so. We must take care that our conduct does not contradict our words; let us be out-and-out Christians, it is much easier than half and half, as well as bringing more glory to God. When we know not the way, let us give God the benefit of the doubt, as dear old Mr. Aitken used to say. Don't say it is not my business to speak; let him that heareth say, Come. If you have heard yourself you are bound to speak to others.' . . . . .

"I think the secret of her power was her deep sympathy; whether it was the death of some beloved relative, or the wish to possess a certain flower, both were remembered and made the subject of prayer. Her humility was most remarkable; she thought every one knew more and was better than herself. Only the last evening I spent with her, she said, 'I shall be a long way from you in heaven.' 'Yes,' I thought, 'but not in the way *you* mean.' The visit of the Bishop, and his prayer that everything might be arranged for her comfort and God's glory, she never forgot, and called him 'the dear Bishop' many times. When the night was dark she used to light two candles and put them in the windows, saying as I came in, 'The lower lights are burning.' Sometimes we did not speak for ten minutes at a time; the being with her and 'resting in her love' did me so much good. . . . . .

"I feel as if I had lost my mother, for she used to tell me what I ought to do, and say she had to take care of my money matters, though assuredly no one *cared* for money less than she did.

"'We loved her well, but Jesus loved her best,' has been my greatest comfort."

---

Miss Mary Tregelles, of Falmouth, another intimate friend, has kindly contributed the following reminiscences in answer to a niece's request:—

"I doubt if any one that did not correspond with that dear saintly aunt of yours would have any idea what beautiful letters she could write; for racy and intensely interesting as her talk was, the words used to be in such a torrent that sometimes one could not remember half that she said; while the beauty and grace of expression in some of her letters showed one much more clearly the renewed spiritual nature, as well as the cultivated mind. . . . . .

"Her letters to me were few, and are not of much general interest, except as showing, as almost every line of hers did, the habitual heavenward attitude of her mind.

"And then her exceeding humility! She always talked of herself as though, in comparison with others, she had only taken the first step in the heavenly path. 'I'm not happy, you know, Mary; I'm not a happy Christian; I don't doubt that my sins are forgiven, but as to *rejoicing!*'—and all the while 'the light that was lit above,' shining out of that beaming face, would assure her listener that peace must flow like a river over her soul, and that she was emphatically one of those 'who carry music in their heart,' and whose 'secret souls a holy strain repeat.' Her habit of constant prayer was no doubt the secret of that heart-music. How very few people in this busy age give so much time to prayer; and how her words used to pour forth! 'There,' she said one day, 'I've tired you to death, I'm sure; but I can't stop you know when I begin, there is so much to pray for.' I was so touched by her telling me not long before her death, that she prayed for me by name every day, amongst a great many other friends, and she seemed surprised at my wondering that she found time in her busy life for such detail.

"I hope somebody will record some of the racy stories with which her talk was interlarded; they were quite too good to be lost, and they often gave such point to the views she was advancing. But how very, very odd some of her sudden ludicrous turns were; as for instance, when she was in full flow once on the subject of baptism by immersion or sprinkling, there was a *sottovoce* aside ('take a lot of water to immerse *me*!') and on she went with her topic. But in her case there never seemed any irreverence; her heart was so centred in all that is highest and best, that the comic interludes which quite upset her listeners scarcely stopped the current of her thoughts for a moment.

...... "Don't you think that whole-hearted devotion to the service of her Lord was her most striking characteristic? Her whole life seemed to breathe the aspiration 'Thy kingdom come, Thy will be *done*,' so earnestly did she set herself to fulfil that Will which with mind and soul she acknowledged to be 'good' and acceptable and perfect.".....

---

Mrs. Aitken's death followed very shortly that of her dear friend; she was then over eighty, and too weak and infirm to write any memoir of Emily Bolitho, but she kindly made a great effort to collect and send the foregoing valuable letters for publication, and with some difficulty recorded one little incident of her friend's frequent visits, as follows:—

"In one of her drives up to Pendeen Miss Bolitho passed along a row of the most recently erected cottages, with pretty gardens in the front of them. She made her driver pause as she was opposite the door of one at which an elderly woman was standing, the mistress of the house, the wife of a most influential Methodist in the parish. Miss Bolitho was looking at her flowers, but the woman was impressed by the singularly bright and happy expression of her countenance, so much so that she retired into the cottage and gave herself to the contemplation (for she well knew who it was) of the circumstances.

'Here is this lady, who has money enough to command the pleasures of this world, renouncing them for the happiness of living and working for Christ; and here am I, a poor old creature, never turned to Christ yet, but seeking my joys in the trash about me;' and this she did, remaining on her knees praying and weeping and pleading till she found peace with God, and was as bright as she who had recently passed, and was for a length of time a faithful attendant at the religious meetings at Pendeen."

Captain Cay (for several years Inspecting Commander of the Coast Guard at Penzance) and his wife were also among her intimate friends. Mrs. Cay writes:—

"I am so sorry that I have only one letter of dear Miss Emily Bolitho's. Had I realised how soon she was to be taken, I should have kept every line I ever received from her.

"During the six years we lived in Penzance we were privileged to see a great deal of Miss Bolitho, and indeed it *was* a privilege—she was always so full of Christ and His work, and so bright and cheerful. I often heard her say 'that dismal Christians were like the spies who brought up a false report of the land.'

"I attended her Bible class whenever my family ties allowed, and always with profit. But the time in which I most heartily enjoyed her society was during 1872 and 1873, when Captain Cay was in the Persian Gulf, and I was alone at Hea Moor with my seven little ones. Often, when lonely and sad, I have gone down the lane to the Coombe, and come back refreshed by a talk and a little prayer with her. Her kindness to me during that solitary time is beyond description; she never failed to come and see me once a week, and if at any time

I was absent from the Sunday or Tuesday evening services, her pony carriage was certain to stop at the door next morning. Such large-hearted sympathy I never met with, and such true *motherly* feeling in a single woman was wonderful. She had ever a kind word for children; I remember so well she took all mine to Prussia Cove for a picnic, and in one of the caves there made them stand in a row and sing Sankey's song, 'The Life-boat.' The morning we left Penzance, though it was only eight in the morning, her dear cheery face was there to see us off, and just before we started she looked into the carriage and said, 'Now let us have *The Life-boat* once more,' and as the children sang it the train moved off, and we never saw her more.

"I think a little circumstance of our first acquaintance is very characteristic of her. Just after my husband's appointment to Penzance the wreck of the *North Briton* occurred, when he narrowly escaped drowning through the life-boat capsizing. On getting home there was just time to change his clothes and be in time for evening service. Miss Bolitho told us, when she came to see us a few days after, that she thought when she saw him come in, 'Well, that new Inspecting Commander must be a duffer!—instead of going to the wreck like a man, he has been taking his ease at home.'. When she knew the facts she came to apologise for her unspoken thoughts.

"I do wish I had anything to send you which would be of use in your book, but Miss Bolitho's work struck me as being of the kind which is not easily chronicled; she just lived and breathed the Spirit of the Master she loved, and I am sure her unconscious influence must have told for good to the many upon whom she brought it to bear. I think, 'Out of the abundance of the heart the mouth speaketh,' most truly applied to her."

Among other friends who saw her less frequently, but fully appreciated her, was Anna Maria Fox, of Penjerrick, Falmouth, who says:—

..... "My visits to her I shall never forget; her graphic histories of how the way was opened for her to visit invalids who came as strangers to Penzance, and whom she longed to help both spiritually and physically. Her warm heart seemed to expand to the whole human race, and her faith was so large in the love of her Heavenly Father that nothing seemed impossible.

"She told me how much she owed to the teaching of Mr. Aitken, of Pendeen, and of the warm friendship which so enriched her life.

"How full of humour she was in her descriptions of various passages in her life which I wish I could remember, but it is only the general impression that is left behind. Her loss must be greatly felt in her own family.

"Do you remember how much she valued meeting the present Bishop of Truro at Penalverne, in 1885, and the very interesting conversation they had when walking in the garden, ending with prayer together before he left?"

---

Mrs. Herbert, wife of the Vicar of St. Peter's, Vauxhall, and an energetic worker for Women's Missions, once stayed at Penzance, when her husband assisted for a short time at St. Paul's. She and Emily Bolitho became very friendly, and for many years after corresponded regularly. She says:—

...... "I wish I could help in preserving a record of dear 'Aunt Emily,' for there is so much self-seeking in even very excellent people, that when one finds a life so wholly given up to God as was hers, it ought to be enshrined, not only in our memories, but in earnest, loving words as a help to those who never knew her in the flesh. I have had a life of such constant occupation for many years, that I cannot trust myself as to *details*, which is what one wants in a Biography, and I recently destroyed all her letters, so that I have only my general recollection of delightful walks with her through the corn-fields, and quiet talks over tea at the Coombe, when she used to eat her frugal crushed biscuit, and pour out a stream of spiritual experience as we talked over some of the difficulties and struggles of the inner life."  . . . . .

---

We have just received, too late for insertion in its proper place, the following letter from her school-fellow,[1] Miss Mary Rogers, late of Penrose:—

"It is a pleasure to be able to contribute ever so little towards a memoir of one for whom I always had such a regard, though the gulf which generally exists between the elders and the younger at school prevents my giving you any special incidents in her life there. Emily was a general favourite at school from her fine honest character and her unfailing spirits and good temper. One reason for our esteem was the cheerful fortitude with which she bore the trying attacks to which she was liable; they would come on quite suddenly,—violent shaking of the head so that it had to be held by some one while the fit lasted; they excited the compassion of all around. I remember the day's pleasure so well described in her letter, and that for an unusual treat my two

[1] See page 7.

elder brothers were invited to join the party from their school at Chudleigh.

"For many years after I left Torre, I saw very little of Emily, but latterly I was more fortunate in meeting her now and then. She never failed to leave behind her a sense of something above this world, and you could see how happy her strong faith and earnest practice made her."

---

During her visits to her niece Mrs. Foster, Emily Bolitho occasionally met Sister Anna, the Superior of St. Faith's, Lostwithiel. She tells us:—

.... "Miss Bolitho always seemed to me to be a true Christian philanthropist. She loved God and her fellow-creatures for His sake; her own soul was a precious jewel entrusted to her care, and she tried to make others value their souls in like manner—not from fear of punishment, but from love to her Saviour and theirs, Who had redeemed them from the enemy at so dear a price. His self-abnegation was her pattern. As she once remarked to me, 'When I read that Herod and his men of war set Him at nought, I feel as if I *can* do and bear anything for Him.'

Though I did not see Miss Bolitho very often, I always thought her a great friend of mine; for when we did meet, it was always a great pleasure to me to converse with her. She first called here on April 1st, 1865, and I once spent a very enjoyable day with her at Penzance, so that our friendship was of long standing, though we did not see much of each other, and never corresponded except on business.". . . .

We have a loving tribute to her memory from one other clergyman, the Rev. A. L. Palmes, Vicar of St. Germans. He was the first Vicar of the new Church of St. John the Baptist, opened in 1881, in which Emily Bolitho took an active interest. A growing need had for some time been felt for an additional church in Penzance, on the eastern side, and by general subscriptions (assisted by a grant from the Ecclesiastical Commissioners) the work was at length accomplished. Among other contributions it was thought well by the family to devote to it the sum of £1,000 which had been bequeathed by the late Miss Bolitho (Mary) for some charitable purpose.

Though Emily Bolitho always remained faithful to her beloved St. Paul's, the nearer situation of St. John's was a great boon to her, especially for the early Celebrations to which she invariably *walked*, though then considerably over sixty years of age. She cordially welcomed and supported the young Vicar in his difficult task of starting the work of a newly-formed parish, where her life-long and intimate knowledge of the people were of great assistance to him. A strong personal friendship with deep spiritual sympathy soon developed between them. He says:—

"I am so glad to hear that you are thinking of putting together a short sketch of one whose memory I prize amongst my most precious possessions.

"If I were asked to summarize the secret of her wide-spread influence, I should say unhesitatingly that it was an intense love of our Lord, and an intense desire to bring others into the same personal contact with Him. Her favorite saint, I have heard her say, was St. Andrew; and I often used to think that her religion was marked by the same beautiful simplicity as his, and the same thirst for the souls of others.

"She taught me, as no one else ever did, the beauty and the necessity of subjective religion, because one felt instinctively that its beauty and its necessity were based upon a real grasp of objective truth.

"She was very fond of hymns, and had a large collection of them gathered from many sources, and made precious to her by various associations; but more precious than them all to her was the hymn of the Incarnation, Mary's *Magnificat*. It was a real experience to her. Her soul did indeed 'magnify the Lord,' and her spirit did indeed 'rejoice in God her Saviour;' and I well remember her saying, though I may not be able to give her exact words, 'Why *should* people set up two systems of religion as if they were antagonistic to one another, whereas they are both parts, and necessary parts, of one great whole. Some people will tell you that religion is an individual thing, others that it is a corporate union of the Church, by first answering the question of personal salvation, just as Mary begins her song in the singular—*My* soul, *my* spirit, *my* Saviour, and ends it in the plural number as she identifies herself with the great host of the redeemed.'

"She was a very constant worshipper at St. John's, and I always felt that the spiritual temperature, so to speak, was somehow higher when she was present, and that her prayers were, as she once expressed it, 'like the arms of Aaron and Hur' to me in my short ministry at Penzance.

"Her union with her Lord brought to her strong emotional nature its own intense suffering as well as its own intense joy. The light of His countenance was in very truth her life— and when for a season it was withdrawn, the 'forsakenness,' as she used to call it, was darkness that might be felt. At such times, like the disciple whom Jesus loved, she lay at His feet as one dead, and then some verse like Isaiah l., 10, or Job xiii., 15, both of them great favorites with her, would come to her with great power, and she would characteristically repeat them aloud with great fervour, wherever she might be.

"She came to the early Celebration at St. John's as long as she was able to walk up the hill from her house, and seemed at such times to be almost caught up to the third heaven, so intense was her own absorption in the presence of her Lord. At such times (and not only at such times, for indeed her face seemed to be habitually lighted up by it) one could literally 'take knowledge of her that she had been with Jesus.' In short, intense realization of His Presence and His Love inspired her whole life, and so made that life an inspiration to others; and I shall ever thank Him from my heart for my short but intimate acquaintance with her here on earth, to be renewed, God grant it! hereafter."

---

Many more such memorials might be given, but these almost form a biography in themselves, and though it has been truly said that "a record of her religious and philanthropic work would fill volumes," it is impossible in this limited space to attempt to add more than a very few details, and to tell briefly how suddenly in the midst of her labors, almost without warning, "she was not, for God took her."

Her careful study of the daily Psalms and Lessons has been already noticed; besides this a large portion of each day was devoted to private meditation and prayer. Wherever she might be staying she invariably retired for an hour's "quiet" either in the afternoon or evening, and in discussing the question of early breakfast she would say it would never suit her to begin her day (*i.e.* have family prayers) before nine o'clock, for she could not possibly do without *two hours* before that for private prayer. If surprise were expressed, she would add in explanation that she had such a long and ever-increasing list of intercessions; and truly it must have been, for the saying quoted by her friend Miss Tregelles, she repeated on all sides—"I always pray for you by name every day." In addition to her ordinary prayers for all relatives and dear friends, many occasional ones were added for persons brought to her notice in any special way. For instance, after General Gordon's death, she said "I do so miss him every day out of my prayers;" and many other cases might be quoted of people in all parts of the world, of whom she had been told, or had read in the newspapers,—the victims of a railway disaster, foreign missionaries, sailors during stormy weather, etc.; or again, for any parish where a Mission was being held, for a Church Congress or Conference, etc.

Perhaps this commencement of her busy day—the laying herself, her work, and all whom she loved before God in prayer, with her subsequent pause "in the midst of the day's turmoil" to turn "aside with Him and rest awhile"—was the key-note of her power over souls. The reflected light from her long communing with her God seemed, as with Moses, to be still illumining her face as she went about her daily tasks or joined in innocent mirth, and showed, as her friend says, "the habitual heavenward attitude of her mind." In illustration of this we give these few pages (alas! the *only* ones found) of her Diary:—

DIARY, 1880. *January 1st, 1.30 a.m.* Just returned from late service at St. Paul's; text—End of all things at hand, 1 Peter, i. Good congregation; fifty communicants. I trust a time of blessing and determination; the future is with God; His grace is sufficient, the Well deep; may I draw more from Him and live for His glory.

Evening; not watchful in conversation, not a profitable day.

*Friday, January 2nd.* Read[1] at Miss Charles's, Call of Samuel, and prayer; took a drive; St. Paul's Christmas Tree; "Friendly" for a short time, Ephes. vi., "Whole Armour" subject.

*Saturday, January 3rd.* Visited sick people at Chyandour; in the afternoon saw Mrs. Rawlings and Hulsman.

*Sunday.* Early Communion at St. Mary's. St. Paul's, noon, Mr. Martyn, Rom. iv. Evening, Isaiah—"Is there not a lie in . . . . right hand." Afternoon, at Class—Epiphany subject. Prayer-meeting in Evening.

*Monday.* G. F. S. Meeting at Miss H——'s; visited in afternoon, saw Maunder.

*January 6th, Epiphany.* St. Mary's, Holy Communion. Oh! may the Holy Spirit, the Star that guides to Jesus lead me more to Him.

DIARY, 1882. *January 1st, 1882.* Brought thus far. At St. John's on New Year's Eve; Mr. Palmes spoke from Deut. viii.— "To humble and to prove," etc., and "Speak to the children of Israel to go forward." After midnight, read Miss Havergal's Consecration hymn: may I know more of its experience, and give up myself more decidedly. At St. John's at 8 a.m., Holy Communion. He alone can be my strength to meet the trials and temptations of the untried future. Called and had prayer with old Mrs. Grantham[2] before service at St. Paul's; had prayer with Mary T—— after service. Meeting at School-room, Luke ii., and Psalm xc., my subject; had a little time of quiet prayer after the people had left. I do thank God that He has

---
[1] She was in the habit of reading once a week to the dressmaker's girls while they sewed.
[2] In addition to many sick and infirm visited in the week, she always read and prayed with one or two *deaf* friends before Church on Sundays.

allowed me to witness for Him there. Oh! may He bless His own word for His glory. Visited some people in village. Went to St. Paul's; Dean Close preached in the morning from Rom. viii.—" He that spared not His own Son," etc.

*Monday.* Wrote poor Mrs. Stephens after Ellen's death; I should like to hear something about that girl's end. Drove E. G—— to Trewidden. Prayer-meeting.[1] I am so sorry there are no general meetings for united prayer.

*Tuesday, January 3rd.* Spent some time at home settling accounts. Read Rom. viii., and had prayer with ——; oh! that he knew the liberty of the Gospel and could trust his Saviour. I wish I were more loving and gentle, and might thus *be an influence*. I saw C. Mann; she says she is trusting. Paid some visits. In afternoon, an hour's talk with Mr. Dusautoy; I think he wants more to rest in a present salvation.

*Wednesday, January 4th.* Read at Miss Charles's; afternoon Bible class,—Luke ii., Matt. ii., the subject. May we all go more to Bethlehem, and return rejoicing and witness to others, and, like the wise men, may Star direct us to Jesus. At G.F.S.[2] spoke on New Year, new life, putting hands into Hand of Jesus; about thirty there; gave cards. May God bless His Word, and keep me very humble.

*January 5th.* Stayed in and read. Called on H. Tyacke; such a patient sufferer. Saw Mrs. Ellis.

*January 7th.* Went to Prayer-meeting. Bible class, Epiphany the subject; gave cards. Oh! may all the members of Bible class know what being kept by the power of God is, and may they all know and follow Jesus.

---

[1] Weekly Prayer-meeting of ladies, held at noon every Monday at R. T. S. depot, which she generally led.

[2] She regularly gave addresses at the weekly classes for the St. Paul's branch of the G.F.S.

*January 8th.* Went to Prayer-meeting; visited in village; dinner at the Coombe with Mr. Roe,—nice conversation and prayer; called on A. A——.

*January 9th.* Went to Prayer-meeting; after dinner left South parade, paid some visits, and came home. Quiet evening, L. White came to talk about Confirmation; Maria G—— and C. Fenton came.

*Sunday, January 11th.* Twenty-two years this day since my dear father died! Oh, how good has God been to me! Visited and had prayer with three before church; Mr. Martyn,—Psalm lxxii.; Holy Communion; Gospel for day, Luke ii.—Jesus in Temple, afternoon subject. Church, evening, Hebrews ii. 5.

*Friday, February 24th, 1882.* Village, morning. Bible-reading by Dean Close, at Lady Hatherton's—"Be careful for nothing," etc. G.F.S., evening; Acts i., subject.

*Saturday, 25th.* Village, morning, very wet; afternoon, Miss H—— came.

I find it too great a task to write daily.

*On Sunday*, Dean Close preached on—If we confess our sins, God is faithful and just to forgive. Visited Mrs. Arnold and Mrs. Grantham before church. Blind man and 1 Corinthians, xiii., afternoon subject. Mount Carmel, in the evening.

*On Monday*, Prayer-meeting. Village, afternoon. Dined at Penalverne.

*Tuesday*, Miss Charles's. Closes here in afternoon, and Martyns, etc.

*Ash Wednesday*, St. John's for early Communion as a strengthener to begin Lent. 11 a.m., Service at St. Paul's; Class afternoon, St. Matt. iv.; Class, evening, Commination Service.

*Thursday*, Village, morning; some calls and church in afternoon. Quiet evening.

To explain her having "left South parade and returned home," we should say that after her father's death she always spent Christmas with her sister Mrs. Walter Borlase and her family,—for many years at Laregan, and after Mr. Borlase's death at 2, South parade, sometimes staying on for three or four weeks. It was a visit she thoroughly enjoyed; her nieces recall especially her interest in the family Bible-reading every morning, and in the repetition of a favorite text by each at the conclusion. Through the day, as her diary shows, she carried on her usual home duties, and then on her return devoted the long winter evenings (with her one hour's exception) to their amusement, either in leading their family games or in reading aloud to them some entertaining story such as Dickens's "Christmas Carol."

Another very favorite visit, almost annual, was to Lanwithan; of this we have already seen something in her letters to Mrs. Foster, who thus beautifully describes her work *there* "for the Master:"—[1]

"When we were children, and often stayed at the Coombe in our grandfather's life-time, Aunt Emily was always the favorite aunt, who made leisure to enter into our joys and interests. As we grew a little older she earnestly sought to lead us on to the life of self-devotion to God; her happy, joyous temper, her perfect sympathy, her utter self-forgetfulness, attracting us to herself and her God.

"After I was married and lived at Lostwithiel, Aunt Emily came to stay with us nearly every year, enjoying and much appreciating the beautifully wooded country around our home. She entered into all our interests,—helping in our night-school and mothers' meetings, and going from day to day to those

[1] See page 150.

who were in sickness or sorrow. Many who are still with us, as well as those who are gone to the Blessed Home, could tell us how much they owe to her spiritual help and prayers.

"Finding how anxious the people were to hear her words of love, we often asked them to come to Lanwithan. I can picture now a lovely summer Sunday evening, the services of the church over, and all the people pouring in at the doors and wide-open windows, till there was hardly standing room, Aunt Emily in the midst singing the singularly appropriate hymn—'Yet there is room;' then followed a fervent address, entreating us to listen to our Saviour's Voice, and closing with—'Shall we gather at the river?'

"Aunt Emily was very shy and humble about these meetings; each was entered into and followed by many earnest prayers and much communing with God; her one desire was to be as the great saint of old, *a voice;* her thoughts expressed in her favourite lines—'Lift up the banner of Thy Cross, and let its folds conceal the standard-bearer.'"

Some of the Bible classes noted in her Diary, and referred to by Mr. R. W. Aitken, Miss Haydon, and Mrs. Cay, she began in Mr. Fenton's time, and continued up to the week of her death with the greatest success. Numbers still speak of them, and dwell gratefully on the lessons learned there; they consisted of a Wednesday afternoon Bible class for educated persons, held in Penzance, and a Wednesday evening and a Sunday afternoon meeting for the poorer class, at Chyandour. These latter, until the Cliff cottages were pulled down in 1874, were held in her school-room on the Cliff; afterwards in Mr. Richard Bolitho's Mission-room at the back of Ponsandane. It was this enforced change of rooms and the destruction of her first meeting-place that she so quaintly describes in one letter as "the gourd that has so long been a blessed shelter and over-shadowing."[1]

The school in Chyandour, founded by her sister Mary, in which she taught as a girl, she kept on (visiting it almost daily) until 1878. The number of children had then become so reduced by the erection of neighbouring Board schools that she felt it to be no longer needed, and took the occasion of her school-mistress's marriage that year to close it.

Besides superintending this school and ministering to all who were sick in Chyandour, she used to visit every house in the village weekly, to change the tracts she was in the habit of lending. It was not such a light task as it sounds, for, as her servant Ann remarked, "She was not one to simply lay down her tract, say 'Good morning,' and pass on;" she must stop to hear all the events, spiritual and temporal, in the family. "She would sit down and be so free—quite as if she were one of us," one poor woman said. Sometimes on returning home tired and late for her dinner, she would say apologetically, "Well, Ann, anyhow I have been able to rejoice with them that do rejoice to-day; so-and-so had had such good news; they were so pleased to tell it me, and I *am* glad for them;" or "I've been allowed to share in *one* sorrow at any rate, to-day; poor so-and-so I found in such trouble. . . . . . I think it was a relief to her to pour it all out to me."

One of her regular duties for many years was taking a month quarterly for visiting the Union Workhouse on Tuesday afternoons; in this she was accompanied by her friend Miss Caroline Carne. She often said these visits depressed her ever more and more. "It isn't only poverty," she would say, "but the mental affliction of so many and the consequences of sin,

[1] See page 88.

and the hopelessness of doing any good." But her sad yearnings over the fallen never hindered her efforts to brighten the lot of the innocent, the aged, and the infirm, and nowhere was her sunny face more eagerly welcomed. Other lady visitors were constantly accosted with—" Have you seen Miss Bolitho lately? Is she very well? We're so longing for her month to come again." Her clear animated singing and reading, her bright smile, her cheery greetings, her bits of news of the outside world, her thoughtful remembrance of the tastes or wants of each, and above all her earnest prayers, made "*her* Tuesdays" indeed "red-letter days" in their poor dull lives. Nor was it merely in the pauper inmates that she interested herself; master, mistress, nurse, porter,—all were included in her friendly sympathy which never seemed to know any barriers of position; its independence of these was shown everywhere. When staying with friends she often astonished mistresses by a knowledge they had never themselves acquired of their servants' inner selves, drawn out in only a few days' opportunity by a kindly word.

In Missionary work of all kinds she took the keenest interest, never failing to attend the annual meetings and services, and begging others to. "I know they are often dull," she would say, "but I think it is our duty to go, for every one that goes or stays away makes *some* difference, and I feel we do do *so little* to strengthen the hands of the Missionaries."

Any new schemes for home mission work too at once claimed her attention. Besides the Girls' Friendly Society she took an active part in superintending the Town Mission, the Maternity Society, and the Rescue Society. At the meetings of this last she would sometimes censure the leniency of the rest of the committee most warmly, and afterwards would whisper aside,

"They all think me very hard, but they are too easily moved to pity; I fear it will be an encouragement to vice if the Society supports such cases; they don't know, as I do, all the particulars;—but here," slipping a coin from her pocket, "you can just give the poor girl this for present relief." Another member, after her death, said, "I can't *think* what we shall do at the Rescue Meetings without her; her judgment was always so excellent, and so quick and decisive, that we all trusted to hers rather than to our own, and her knowledge of the people and clear recollection of all their circumstances were safe to be relied on."

Though, apart from her religious studies, not a great general reader, she much appreciated an amusing tale, a biography, or Missionary history. For many years she was Treasurer of the Ladies' Reading Society, of which her sister Mrs. Grenfell was President, chose the books and generally read them before they were circulated; but she preferred sharing the enjoyment of a good story with others; she had an excellent voice, and would read aloud for hours together without apparent fatigue.

It has been well said that "all natures gifted with wide and generous sympathies have a fund of humour, and indeed a vein of pure and healthy fun;" and that "the deepest, purest characters are also the swiftest in sympathy with the startling strands of humour which are interwoven with our sad and mysterious life." Certainly Emily Bolitho was no exception to this, and many regret that this notable feature in her character is so little represented in her letters, and have begged that some of her humorous stories and quick repartees might be chronicled, but it is a hard task.

We agree with the recent biographer of a celebrated wit, that "Perforce what is written down and has to be read out of a printed book is so utterly unlike what was brilliantly and effectively spoken—came all alive, so to speak, from the brain which gave it birth, and was attended by the joyous laughter of appreciative friends. . . . . . What need to add that every several gem, divested of its *setting*, no longer sparkles as at the first? It was not only the suddenness of the saying, but its aptness to what had just gone before which delighted; divorced from its context it loses more than half its charm."

One or two examples, however, may serve to recall better ones to those who knew her. Hearing a description of the arrangements of a clergy-house—the clergy cleaning and dusting their own rooms, etc.—she exclaimed, "And you do all that yourselves Canon C——!" "Yes, and sing the while 'Angels hovering round.'" "Well, I don't know about the *angels*, but there's *certain* to be *dust* 'hovering round' if you have no woman at work!"

She often in fun quoted the expression of an old servant, who, when engaged to be married, was asked if she were very happy, and replied, "Oh, yes, we gets on very comfortable; there ain't no *rapshurs*, you know!"

Once when being taken into dinner by a young man who had just come into a large fortune, she exclaimed as he offered her his arm, "This is quite a case of the Baroness Burdett Coutts reversed!"

A favorite anecdote was of a young clergyman, a stranger, visiting one of the old-fashioned country churches, and being conducted round by the old pew-opener. Rather scandalized at the bye-gone ideas of services, etc., he said, "And pray, my good woman, do you not have Mattins?" "Well, no sir, I can't say we have got no *mattin*, but we have Linoleum right up to the Altar-steps!"

Another was of a friend who, on going to see a poor old woman, congratulated her on the blessing of being able to read her Bible. "Yes, indeed, God's Word is my meat and drink, and my light by night, for I'm *resting on the promises*. "Well, I'm very glad to hear it, you will find true comfort always in doing that." "Yes, that I do; for I'm thinking of that old rascal of a husband of mine, and I read 'vengeance is Mine, *I* will repay,' saith the Lord; so I know he'll be served out some day!"

Perhaps her best-known stories were the adventures of Capt. Oates,[1] and the mention of these brings before our eyes the bright happy scenes in which she was wont to repeat them, surrounded by an ever-freshly delighted group of merry young listeners;—we mean the Coombe tea-parties.

The Coombe had always been famed for its hospitality, and Emily Bolitho well maintained the reputation of the old home, which no one ever visited without the kindest reception from her; but in the days when she first took her stand as an earnest worker for God, such a course meant almost entire severance from the world and its pleasures, so that the brilliant social gifts which might otherwise have made her a leader of society were chiefly expended on the entertainment of the young, and nowhere did they shine out more strongly than at these gatherings of her brothers' and sisters' families. As children, their earliest recollections of such parties were those on May-day mornings, when they were invited to breakfast, all wearing garlands of flowers; the happy day commencing with singing the Morning Hymn—"Awake my soul," and "Aunt Emily" reading the Epistle and Gospel for the day (St. Philip and St. James); and after breakfast all dancing with her

---

[1] As told by Mr. G. Hicks, of Bodmin.

round the May-pole on the lawn, and playing various games. Her illness in the spring of 1875 made a break in this annual custom; and as the children were then mostly grown up, she in after years changed the party into an evening one. She also gave one for her birthday (October 11th), and occasionally at other times of the year, and never was any festivity more thoroughly enjoyed; all seemed to allow themselves to be carried back to the days of their childhood, as did "Aunt Emily" herself; and even to those who had entered the family too late for the enrichment of these early associations, the Coombe parties were unique in their simple gaiety, and all threw themselves unreservedly into the spirit of fun and freedom that always reigned. All appreciated her bright loving welcome, her special word for each, her wonderful knack of reaching and keeping all within the radius of her kindly mirth; the playful ceremony with which, in the usual dearth of gentlemen, girls were paired off together to follow her into the dining-room and ranged down each side of the long-stretched tea-table, laden with the most tempting home-made dishes; her alertness in reviving conversation, if it ever flagged during the festive meal; the careful attentions of her two devoted servants Ann and Christopher, entering as heartily as herself into the hospitable entertainment of her guests. Then, tea over, the general rush out,—in summer to walk and sit in the dear old garden, in winter to surround her in the drawing-room with ardent clamour for "Aunt Emily's stories," or "Aunt Emily's" games of "Family coach," "My ship comes home,", "Thoughts," etc., at which none could equal her in readiness of reply. No children's birthday-party or Christmas-tree or School-treat was given in the family without "Aunt Emily" must of necessity be there to lead the amusements; to dance with the children "round the mulberry bush" was one of her favorite games. . . . None were ever too young for her; from earliest babyhood to maturity each was to her "a dear child," and in their eyes she never could be too old to be their boon companion. After a visit to Lanwithan, not long before her death, a poor woman asked "When the *dear old lady* was coming again?" Her niece quite startled, replied, "Why, Aunt Emily is *not old!*" and then remembered that in *years* she was actually over 65. For those of her family older and more infirm than herself her anxious care was unceasing; many will remember the familiar sight of her in her low pony-carriage driven by her faithful Christopher, taking her sister almost daily for a morning drive, and paying affectionate calls at the different relations' houses.

Her health had all her life been wonderfully good, nor, with the exception of scarlet fever when a girl, and the successful operation in 1875, had she ever had any serious illness. She hardly comprehended that age must lessen her labors, and still struggled bravely on at both mental and physical work with efforts far beyond her strength, though often complaining of painful indigestion and nervous exhaustion. The only infirmity which really hindered her latterly was failure of sight. Doctors pronounced it a hopeless case, failure of nerve-power in the eyes as well as cataract. To one so quick and active-minded it was becoming daily more and more trying to be dependent on others for reading or writing, and latterly even for recognizing people. The burning pain in her eyes made her shun any strong light, and the last year or two she would often spend her evenings without lamp or candle, sitting alone in the darkness. "But I have such happy times," she used to say; "Thank God, I can feel that He is there with me; and *I just talk to*

*Him* and tell Him all that troubles me." She generally had by her side in these dark hours a little luminous cross of which she was very fond, and once after hearing an earnest evangelical sermon delivered against the use of the emblem of the cross, she said, "I think if the preacher could know what marvellous thoughts that little cross brings to me as I sit alone in the dark, he would be more lenient, though God forbid that I should ever regard it idolatrously."

The Bishop of Truro, who had been staying in the house with her only three weeks before she died, in a kind note of sympathy afterwards to her brother, said, "That it had been a confirmation of his own faith to meet one whose love to Christ was so strong that it enabled her to face with resignation such a heavy trial as her approaching blindness." Her admiration of his teaching we have already seen in her account of their meeting at Pendeen,[1] and this had been further increased when staying with him at her nephew Mr. Robins Bolitho's.[2] In December, 1885, he was coming to hold a special Confirmation at the newly-built Mission Church of All Saints', Trythall; he was to be the guest of her niece Mrs. John Bolitho, and she gladly accepted an invitation to meet him, little thinking it was to be for the last time. How greatly she enjoyed this intercourse with him, and how amidst the pleasure of her visit the one chief desire of her soul was still uppermost in her mind (see her last letter to Miss M. Tyacke, page 150), is best given in the words of her niece's diary:—

*Trevaylor, November, 1885.* Directly I knew for certain that the Bishop was coming, I asked Aunt Emily to stay with me to meet him. I was so afraid she might be engaged, but she did not hesitate at all,—said she should enjoy coming to meet

[1] See page 132.  [2] See page 160.

him above everything; her only fear she might be taking up the room of somebody more important; and whenever I have met her since, she has always said, "Now mind, Elsie my dear, you are not to think of me; if there is any one else you want to ask, don't scruple to put me off, I shall be quite content." She constantly impressed on me not to put myself out for her, she could sleep anywhere, etc.; and from fear of giving trouble I had great difficulty to persuade her to bring Ann.

*November 30th, St. Andrew's Day.* I met Aunt Emily coming out of St. Mary's; she said she was too busy really to afford the time to come to church, but she was "so fond of St. Andrew, she could not make up her mind to miss him over!"

She agreed to come up with Ann about tea-time next day to begin her visit; with her constant thoughtfulness begged me not to hurry back from Trythall, where she knew I should be busy decorating the church for the Confirmation.

*Tuesday, December 1st.* It happened that I *was* detained late, and found her on my return home comfortably settled in the school-room, amusing Evelyn with all kinds of stories. After tea she asked Miss Burton (the governess) to read to her while Evelyn was with me; when he went back to his lessons again she came down in the drawing-room, and both before and after supper we put aside the lamp and sat together in the firelight, and she talked most wonderfully and prayed with me. I read her the Evening Lessons, and she had so many nice thoughts on them.

*Wednesday.* Aunt Emily was down to prayers at eight o'clock. When we read the Psalm she repeated it by heart with us (she could not see to read); afterwards she prayed aloud for all. After breakfast came to Bible-reading in school-room.

First Lesson, Isaiah xxii.; the verse—"He will surely violently turn and toss thee as a ball into a large country"—she explained to Evelyn meant a peculiar kind of plant that rolled over and acquired nourishment as it turned; the Second Lesson in St. John she knew so well that she would repeat her verse in turn. The Bishop came in the afternoon, and drove up to Trythall for Confirmation; forty candidates—many of them old people. Aunt Emily and all of us went, and enjoyed the service greatly; the Bishop said afterwards that he had too. In the evening a few of the family and the Vicar came to dine; Aunt Emily looked particularly nice, and seemed very happy.

*Thursday, December 3rd.* Quiet day for the clergy. Aunt Emily and I went in with the Bishop to St. Mary's, and remained for Holy Communion, and heard his first address; she went thence to the Coombe, and drove back here with him in the evening.

*Friday, 4th.* The Bishop left for Trengwainton after Confirmation at St. Mary's in the afternoon. Aunt Emily delighted with his visit; "He *leavens* his conversation so with good," she said. "If asked what I think of him, I shall say, 'He is a *courteous Christian* gentleman;' there is no doubt that is what he is."

*Sunday, December 6th.* Aunt Emily went home over-night to prepare for her Sunday work. I called at the Coombe for her in the evening, and drove her to St. John's to hear the Bishop preach. We went early to get a chance of good seats, and I thought she was comfortably established in one, when to my dismay I saw her leave it to insist on its being occupied by a deaf servant whom she had spied further off. "My dear, it is of far more consequence for *her* to be near the pulpit than me," she whispered. However, happily we got her the next place. There being yet some time before the service began, she begged me to read her in a whisper the Gospel for the day and Miss Havergal's Advent Hymn—"Thou art coming, O my Saviour" (which was afterwards sung). The Bishop's text was—"The love of Christ constraineth us." He said this had two meanings in the Greek,—firstly, the *supporting*, as with iron bands, anything likely to fall to pieces; secondly, the *bounding in*, as rocks a stream, forcing it forward in a narrow, direct channel. He spoke of conversion of St. Paul. Scene:—dusty plain and snowy peak of Hermon in the distance; his heart pure as snow in the eyes of man, but dry as the sandy dust in the eyes of God; described how utterly changed by the constraining love of Christ. Aunt Emily pressed my arm, murmuring "How *lovely!*"

*Monday, 7th.* Went with Aunt Emily to St. Paul's at three o'clock to hear Bishop preach again, on Isaiah lxiii. 1.—"Who is this that cometh. . . . . . mighty to save?" Strong Son of God, Conqueror; fought the battle for us, now *sat down* to receive glory and worship. . . . . .

We all went back to tea at the Coombe.

*Wednesday 9th.* Aunt Emily drove up to Carfury with me, and spoke at my mothers' meeting; twenty-six women came. She talked of the coming of the Lord, and being ready for Him; none of us knew but what this might be the last Advent we should be here. He said, "Surely I come quickly;" and we ought to be able to pray, "Even so, come Lord Jesus." She appealed to them all most earnestly each to ask themselves whether they were prepared for this. The mothers seemed deeply impressed: one afterwards recalled a former address of Aunt Emily's to them, in which she said "*she* had driven up comfortably in Mrs. John Bolitho's carriage, but she thought as she rode along how differently her Saviour had travelled—footsore and weary, parched with thirst."

*Sunday, December 13th.* Took Aunt Emily to St. John's Evening Service (she had gone home again for her Sunday classes, etc.) At prayers here she spoke so nicely on Malachi iii., a refiner sitting to sift and judge.

*Tuesday, December 15th.* Aunt Emily left; obliged to return home because expecting Cissy Fenton to stay with her before she starts for China. (She talked a great deal of this Chinese Mission, anxious about Cissy, but dwelling much on the importance of the work.)

*Monday, 21st, St. Thomas's Day.* Drove Aunt Emily home from her Prayer-meeting at Miss Harvey's after church.[1] She spoke again on the beautiful lesson of the Collect, *his* doubts being allowed for the confirmation of *our faith*. In the afternoon Aunt Emily came up here with R. and A. to tea. All went up in school-room. Aunt Emily said, "quite nice to be back again!". . . . . .

Thus far her niece's diary. With this drive to Trevaylor ended her last day in health. The week since her return home had been fully occupied with Christmas preparations. Her gifts were far too numerous to admit of their being costly in *money,* but a wealth of time and trouble was expended on them, for not a single friend was forgotten, and every card even was prayed over and studied to suit individual tastes, and always accompanied by a loving inscription, if not a letter. [By a strange Providence, one might almost call it, she had this year had her photograph taken, purposely to be her Christmas present to all her relatives and friends—*see frontispiece*.] The laborious amount of writing this entailed was now far beyond

[1] See page 142.

the powers of her failing sight, but with the willing help of some of her nieces she got all inscribed and addressed ready for despatch, with one exception;—this little unfinished note, to her old friend Miss Fanny Grenfell, was found in her writing portfolio after her death :—

"The Coombe, *Christmas, 1885.*

"My dear Fanny,—I feel sure you will be pleased to receive the enclosed. Twenty-three years ago I was taken, and now as an old woman I thought I had better once more go through that ordeal.

"I cannot see in detail the likeness, but I do pray that His image may be more stamped upon me and reflected by me, and may He make the coming Season one of sacred, holy joy. I must not write more.

"I have been staying at Trevaylor with my niece Mrs. J. Bolitho. Our dear good Bishop was our guest there for two days; he was delightful."

This characteristic last prayer was fully answered: for herself "the coming season" was indeed to be "one of sacred, holy joy;" and those who received the invaluable token, so speedily followed by the news of their friend's death, as they lovingly gazed at the faithful likeness seemed to see more and more of "His image stamped upon" the dear face.

Another arduous business was the inscribing a text on a motto-card for each member of her Bible class. The choice of this text she always made a matter of most earnest prayer, and then opened her Bible and at once fixed upon and wrote down the one to which she believed herself guided. "Ye are my witnesses, saith the Lord," was the text one year, and another, "I will help thee, saith the Lord;" another, "Surely I will be with thee."

On January 1st, 1886, the New Year's cards she had as usual so carefully prepared were sent round, and her last Bible word—"The Lord giveth wisdom"—came as a message of comfort from another world to the many loving followers to whom it seemed, as to Elisha of old, that the Lord had indeed "taken away their master from their head that day."

The morning of Tuesday, 22nd, she spent in the village distributing almanacks to every house. She returned to dinner at two o'clock, ate it with a good appetite, and drove out afterwards with Miss Fenton, telling Ann not to expect them back till nine o'clock, as they were going to church. She had helped to get Mr. Rudall, a former Vicar of St. Paul's, to come and preach that evening, so was particularly anxious not to miss the service; and they had arranged after separating to call on different friends in the town, to meet again at tea at Mrs. Borlase's before church. Not long before the hour for service she left her friends the Miss Tyackes, to whom some of her last words were, "I do really, *really* believe I shall go blind;" adding more calmly, "Still others have become blind as well as me, and if it is to be so, no doubt grace will be given me to bear it." She complained then of great exhaustion and weariness, but no one thought it more than the natural result of her long, fatiguing day. By the special leading, it would seem, of an Unseen Hand, as she went out into the dark street she unexpectedly met Miss Fenton, and was able to have the guidance of her arm as she bent her wearied steps down Clarence street to the R.T.S. Depôt, where she rested a few minutes, and after exchanging a friendly greeting with Miss Harvey went on towards South parade.

Before reaching the middle of the town she was seized with a sudden giddiness, and had it not been for Miss Fenton's support must have fallen. She was assisted into a chemist's shop, and as soon as she had a little recovered, taken home in a cab. Great was her servant's surprise and consternation at seeing her return thus early, still greater to hear her say in a feeble voice, "Get me into the dining-room, Ann; *I'm dying.*" · Hardly had she reached it when violent sickness overcame her, followed by a long attack of faintness. The doctor was quickly fetched, but for some time could not succeed in rallying her strength: when, however, at last they got her to bed, she became more comfortable and slept a little. The next morning, when Miss Fenton was obliged to leave (to embark for China), she was thought better, but the feeling of nausea always continued, and prevented her ever eating solid food; and the doctor pronounced the action of her heart to be so feeble and intermittent that "a sudden turn in the bed might stop it" (which was what must have actually occurred at the last).

On Christmas Day she had the cards and presents sent by different friends shown her, and was pleased as usual with their kind remembrance, though hardly able to rouse herself to look at them. Her prostration was so great, that when Mr. Hunt called to offer the Holy Communion, she said, No, she must wait a little longer; she could not bear it yet. Ann once remarked, "Why how is it, Miss Bolitho, you're not so much for praying or Bible-reading as usual?" "No, I feel I've no power now to pray," was the answer. "*I must simply leave it all in God's hands.* If ever I live to go about the village again I will try to impress upon them, more strongly than ever, that it's no use to wait until you are dying to prepare for death."

It was a remarkable comment on her life, which had been almost one continuous prayer, that now in the hour of danger, when many would have been making anxious struggles to pray, she could calmly and silently "rest in the Lord."

Her niece, Carrie Borlase, and one or other of the sisters were always with her. On the evening of Tuesday, 29th, she seemed decidedly better, so much so that when the doctor came about eight o'clock, he gave leave for her to be moved into another room next day if she continued as well. She had seen several of the family in the afternoon, and was not apparently the worse for it; and later on had had the Psalms and some of her favorite hymns read to her. During the night she twice asked for beef-tea, begging Ann at the same time to "make a cup of tea for herself!" All through her illness Ann said she overpowered her with grateful thanks for every little service rendered. "Oh you *are so* good to me," she would say, "and every one shows me so much kindness; I feel *full* of thankfulness." In the morning (30th) when Ann had given her her cup of tea and settled her comfortably, her mistress with her never-failing thoughtfulness for others begged her to leave her and go down and see to Miss Borlase's breakfast. "I'm afraid poor little Miss Carrie's neglected, you're so taken up with me." Ann hesitated to leave her, but seeing she really wished it, went, and as she passed along the passage heard her say in a loud, clear voice, "Praise the Lord! O praise the Lord." On reaching the kitchen Ann exclaimed, "Well, Miss Bolitho is certainly better, for I've been sent out of the room for her to say her prayers, and she is now praising the Lord aloud quite like her usual self." A messenger from one of the family had then arrived with enquiries, and bringing a bunch of violets. Knowing Miss Bolitho's fondness for these flowers, Ann, dismissing the man with the message that "Miss Bolitho had had a good night and was very comfortable," hastened upstairs at once with the bouquet, intending to set it down silently without interrupting. In doing so, a glance towards the bed showed her Miss Bolitho's face turned round (it had before been turned towards the wall), and such a change passing over it that she rushed to support her, crying, "My dear Miss Bolitho, you're faint." Her mistress gave one look, one long breath, and without a pang or struggle her spirit returned to God Who gave it. He had mercifully spared her the physical pain of death, her dread of which had always been a trouble to her, partly from fear that it betokened a want of faith; spared too what seemed the inevitable trial of blindness, just when her submission to it was complete. All unperceived His angel came in one swift moment to interrupt the song of praise then on her lips by summoning her to continue it in her Master's presence.

In the days that followed, those privileged to look on her beloved face could hardly believe in the presence of death; the calm happy expression, the still bright color were so life-like; one only seemed to feel that the words so often in her thoughts and on her lips were now a realized *fact*:—

> "Safe in the arms of Jesus,
> Safe on His gentle breast,
> There by His love o'ershaded
> Sweetly my soul shall rest."

One friend wrote, "Indeed the news *is* startling; but over-powering all is the thought of what a happy New Year for her; what happy meetings with those gone before! Yes, truly, *can* we grieve for her? Anything but rejoicing seems out of place in thinking of her; but for those left! What *will* Penzance do without her?"

Great indeed was the sorrow and consternation among both rich and poor. In Chyandour, as one inmate graphically expressed it, "*the village stood still*," mute, paralyzed under the shock of its loss; and when the day of the funeral was fixed, the men all came forward entreating to be allowed to carry her coffin; and so from the dear old Coombe, the home she loved so well, through the village she had tended all her life her body was borne to its last resting-place beside her parents in Gulval churchyard, by the loving hands of those among whom and for whom she had so faithfully labored.

In spite of a continuous downpour of rain the funeral was attended by hundreds, of all classes; the church and churchyard were full to overflowing, and rarely had been seen such an assemblage of aged and poor as struggled to pay this last token of grateful respect to her memory.

Some of her favorite hymns were sung; the St. Paul's choir coming to assist that of Gulval. Never more appropriate seemed the beautiful one of Lyte's—"For ever with the Lord," after the Lesson, and "Safe in the Arms of Jesus" sung as the body was carried from the church to the grave. After the coffin, almost hidden in the masses of beautiful white wreaths, had been lowered, and all were crowding around for one last look, came as an up-lifting of hope the familiar strains of

"Jesus lives! no longer now
Can thy terrors, Death, appal us."

One who was present wrote, "*After* 'the strife is o'er, the battle won,' one turns to the friends, and one thinks of you in the great loss we have sustained; to you it must be a *great* loss. As we were going away from the open grave there seemed no complaint possible; still it does seem hard to think we are no longer to see that kind face, that warm shake of the hand and those many self-forgetting little actions."

Numberless almost were the letters and expressions of sympathy received by her relatives. Some of the Bishop's kind words respecting their recent meeting we have already given; he also wrote by his chaplain to another of the family, "You have the Bishop's heartfelt sympathy and prayers;" and again, "His sympathy with you all is very great, though perhaps few have such strong consolation as you all have in knowing that it is a saint who has gone to rest, whose work on earth has left behind sweet and holy memorials of a 'fellow-worker with God.'"

Her old friend Miss Fanny Grenfell wrote thus to one of the sisters :—

"I was much pleased to get a letter from you, and thank you much for the simple memorial card of your dear sister. I do not wonder at your lamenting her loss as you do. I know what a comfort she must have been to you, and her visits must be *sadly* missed. I miss her much in my thoughts; for though separated from her society so many long years—weary ones mostly to me—she never forgot me; especially after the few years I spent at Penzance five-and-twenty years or so ago, when we had not met for ages, as you know, and we had, as it were, to renew the friendship, both changed in many ways not necessary to account for, and yet her open-hearted kindness soon broke the ice that had almost formed over it by that time, and soon I found the *old* friend in the new one; only there was also the development into a bright and benevolent Christian woman—all her energies turned into one direction—whom no one, even if they did not agree in all respects with the line she took, could but admire and be influenced in some manner by her spirit of love and beaming charity embracing so many different characters, and so free from the littlenesses of ordinary women, and so uncompromising in following out whatever she was convinced was her duty, and so unwearied and unselfish and with such power of sympathy.

"After a bad illness I had, she made me come and be nursed into convalescence at the Coombe,—of course making it a time for speaking as she might of the theme so near her heart. She always had great influence with me, and at any rate her conversations tended to warm my colder heart in some measure, though I might not eventually agree with her views; and I shall never forget those few weeks, and her devotion to your father,—it was about a year, I think, before his death. From that time to this, after I left Penzance she never failed to write from time to time; would send me a little present on my *birthday* (seldom referred to by any one else), and always at Christmas. I am glad to think she wrote to me (almost illegibly) only a few days before her *going home*, with what she knew would please me—*her* photo and that of the dear old Mount, a *few* lines hard to make out. It is short and interrupted,[1] but characteristic, and to me very precious; it shows that with failing powers—for she must have been ill then—her heart was true and constant as ever.

"Yes, it was a blessed end for her, and the *joy* so suddenly granted in unconsciousness—fancy it one can't! and a fitting reward for her bright trust in Him Whom I always think she may have *seen* just as those last characteristic words were heard from her lips, when, no earthly friend at the moment was near.". . . . .

[1] Page 184.

Her old friend Mrs. Aitken, in spite of age and infirmity, wrote in her own hand these few touching lines:—

"Thank you so much, my dear C., for your kindness in letting me hear, as God's dealings with her were carried on, the details of the last days of our blessed saint.

"Precious Emily! She must be missed; and who can fill her place? But her work is finished, and she is called to rest and to the vision of Him whom she supremely loved.

"Oh that those for whom she prayed and labored may walk in the light that guided her, and rest not until they are made partakers of her undying joys!"......

Mrs. Close, the widow of Dean Close, who during several winter visits to Penzance had had much friendly intercourse with her, wrote to one of her nieces:—

...... "I long to say to you how very deeply I sympathize with you and all your family in the great loss you have all sustained in the removal of dear Miss Bolitho. She was so largely valued and loved, as she well deserved to be. For myself, the thought of my visit to dear Penzance has lost, oh! so much of its attraction; her loving welcome, her affectionate greeting, her varied and agreeable converse, and above all, her spiritual teaching made it such a pleasure when her name was announced as coming in for a quiet talk, as she did often during my last visit to Lady Hatherton...... Dear M—— will feel her loss greatly; indeed, who will not? The *poor poor*—what will they do without her tender sympathy, her helpful prayers?

"For *her* we rejoice; and life would have been trying if her sight had grown weaker. Our God has taken her where she will be *fully* satisfied......

"There was so much of originality of thought and of deep spirituality, combined with such constant painstaking kindness to all, and warm love to her friends, that she must live in the memory and heart of all who had the real privilege of knowing her. We shall meet again shortly, as my eighty years tell me constantly, and in the presence of Him whom she loved and served faithfully.". . . . .

Mr. J. Pethybridge, late manager of the East Cornwall Bank, Bodmin, whom she had often visited from Lanwithan, and particularly in the beginning of his last illness, wrote from Madeira to her brother thus:—

"Last week's mail brought me your very kind note of the 24th December, which did me good. . . . . . The absence of 'mourning' you referred to, in the past year, I see by the Penzance paper is now broken by the death of dear Miss Emily Bolitho. Her Christian life was eminently a bright and happy one, and her labors for the good of others were unceasing. I and my family will always remember her last visit to us at the Bank, when she offered an earnest prayer to God for His rich blessings on us all. 'The memory of the just is blessed;' and truly she will ever be remembered by hundreds of the rich and the poor, and deeply will her loss be felt by those to whom for so many years she was wont to minister spiritual as well as earthly comfort. 'Precious in the sight of the Lord is the death of His saints!' Her happy spirit has joined the great family above, and one more is added to the number of those whom we hope to meet again, and perhaps at no distant time. By God's grace may we, like the dear departed one, be found ready and waiting the coming of our Lord.". . . . . .

On the granite cross that marks her grave, beneath the simple record of her name, age, and birthplace, is inscribed her favorite text—"When I awake up after Thy likeness I shall be satisfied."

At St. Paul's a subscription was at once started towards some memorial of her, which it was decided should take the form of a porch to the church. This was felt to be in accordance with a frequently expressed desire of hers to increase the space, and lessen the draught for worshippers at the bottom of the church. On a large brass tablet within is this inscription:—"To the glory of God, and in thankful memory of Emily Borlase Bolitho, this tablet and memorial porch are erected by loving friends and members of this congregation. 'After she had served her own generation, by the will of God she fell on sleep' 30th December, 1885."

---

Preaching in St. Paul's Church on the Sunday after her death, the Vicar (the Rev. J. J. Hunt) taking for his morning text 1 Thess. iv., 14, remarked that the bright hope of the Lord Jesus Christ coming again with His departed saints, came before them that morning with special emphasis as they thought of her who had just been taken from amongst them to her heavenly rest. It was very hard to realise that she was gone. It was as though a wound had opened out in their midst; as though a part of the church itself had gone. Early led to her Saviour under that devoted servant of God, Mr. Aitken, of Pendeen, she had looked upon her conversion not merely as an escape from hell, but as the commencement of a life to be wholly lived for her Master. From that time forth she had completely given up herself to Him. How she had loved their little church! How she had become a part and parcel of it; entering into all the spiritual work carried on in connection with it! What a friend and helper she had been of its various ministers! Then how great was her humble-mindedness! No one had a greater sense of her personal shortcomings. No one more deprecated every word said in her praise. Always lamenting her want of faith, her whole life was one of faith from first to last. Continually bemoaning how little she did, her life was one long sacrifice of herself for the good of others.

And then her motive power! What an exalted one it was. Just this: love to Christ; and then as a natural consequence, love to those around. This love led her to be in very deed instant in season and out of season. Her time was her Master's; her Master's time was hers. She was ever seeking for opportunities of doing good. And it came so naturally to her to speak for Jesus, whether amongst the poor, or amongst those of her own position in life. With her it was the most natural thing to draw the conversation to holy things. How many could bear testimony to the good received from her.

She never knew what is commonly called the domestic joys of home life, but she left a large family behind her, a family of those all over the neighbourhood to whom she had so lovingly ministered in every circumstance of life; above all of those whom she had been made the means of leading to the feet of Jesus. And this her loving sympathy had grown to be part of her being. The preacher did not know how it seemed to others, but to him it always appeared, not so much that she had peculiar gifts of sympathy which were not possessed by others, but that she had gazed so continually into the face of her Saviour, and had drunk in so much of His love, that as a natural consequence that love flowed out to those about her. Then, how tender she was in conscience. If at any time she thought that a word of hers might have given unintentional pain, how she would reproach herself, and never rest until she had sought out the one she thought she had wounded, and told how grieved she was.

How great, too, was her love of prayer! This necessarily grew from her love to Christ; loving Him—she loved to hold communion with Him. Nor was it for herself alone she prayed. It was wonderful the number of those for whom she made supplication daily before the Throne of Grace. The last great day alone would reveal how much blessing had as a consequence of these prayers descended upon her church and its respective ministers. How great, too, was her love for the house of God! How seldom, notwithstanding increase of age, was her place vacant there. Often had the preacher entering the church half-an-hour or more before service, found her already there, alone with God. In common with many other servants of God, she had a natural physical shrinking from the approach of death (not from its consequences, her feet were too firmly grounded upon the rock Christ Jesus to admit of that; but from the act of death itself). She often used to speak of her old friend and father-in-Christ, Mr. Aitken; of the sudden way in which he had been called from earth to glory, and of what a blessed change it was for him. And God was equally gracious to her. Hers was not death, but a translation. She was not, for God took her. Her last words, overheard in an adjoining room when there was no thought that her end was approaching, were, "Praise the Lord." Shortly after, she was found by her attendant in a state of unconsciousness. A tremour of the eye, a faint beat of the pulse, and all was over. She had passed away from earth to the presence of the Lord she loved and served so well. In her death were fulfilled the words of one of her favourite texts, one which with many others sanctified the walls of her room—" I will both lay me down in peace and sleep, for Thou, Lord, only makest me dwell in safety." Calmly she lay down in perfect peace, and the Lord had made her to rest in safety with Him for evermore. Her life (long, not so much in years as in deeds) over, she had gone to join the ranks of those who had first been privileged to start her in and to help her along the heavenly way, in whose footsteps she had followed, and whose memory she had revered and loved so well.

In conclusion, the preacher addressed a special word to the younger members of the congregation. Did they wonder at that noble life and that happy death? Did they as they witnessed all the tokens of sorrow around find a longing arise in their hearts that such a well-spent life and happy departure might be theirs; and did they at the same time feel disposed to think that such longings must all be vain, that they were setting before themselves an ideal it would be impossible to realise,—he would remind them that it was not so. It was not that she whose departure they mourned was naturally an uncommon woman. She was one of like passions with them. She knew the same temptations, she groaned under the same sense of her own failures; but the secret of her power was this—that she gave her heart to Jesus, and having taken Him as her Saviour, henceforth delivered up her whole self to be led and used by Him. Let them remember that although she, it was true, had gone, her Master yet remained. What he had done in her, He could and would do in them. Let them on this the first Sunday of a new year, set out, looking to God alone for grace, with this determination, that come what might, they would be wholly His. Let them make trial of His love and power, and prove what He would do in them. Like her they would have many sore temptations; they might have to mourn over many failures; but He Who had manifested His faithfulness to her would do the same to them; and when at length the time should come when they too should depart this life it would be given to them to know that their life had not been wholly spent in vain, but that they had been privileged to do something at any rate for Him Who had done so much for them.

---

We feel that no words of ours can so fully epitomize what has gone before, or so well conclude this little memoir, as these touching verses which appeared in the Penzance evening paper the day of her funeral, January 2nd, 1886:—

> GONE, from the old sequester'd vale,
>   Gone, from the home beside the sea,
> No longer can'st thou hear the tale,
>   "Lady, the poor man wanteth thee."
> Where in the narrow darkened room,
>   Thine hand hath smoothed the quilted bed,
> For thee, dear lady of the Coombe,
>   The sick one's silent tear is shed.
>
> And where from cottage, dank and foul,
>   Thy word the demon Drink has driven,
> And set the parched and weary soul
>   Athirst for the pure founts of Heaven.
> There too (now all is neat and trim),
>   The wife and husband weep for thee,
> Who taught *her* patience, rescued *him*,
>   And brought their children round his knee.

## REMINISCENCES.

Not far from hence, 'mid kith and kin,
  Where riches reign in bounteous hall,
When Yule-tide made light hearts within,
  Thine was the lightest of them all.
The tears of youth,—the sighs of age,—
  The passing thoughts that prompted fear,
Each joy and sorrow on life's page
  Alike found refuge in thine ear.

So loving, loveable, beloved,—
  Sincere and simple in thy ways,—
The better life thy life has proved
  The simpler life of elder days.
In thee, did sympathy combine
  With all-enduring trust in God,
So that in faith thou could'st resign
  Thyself to His all-chastening rod.

Brave soul and noble; like the rock
  That stems the surge at Chyandour,
On thee,—unconscious of the shock,
  The waves of evil spent their power:
There, hard beside the Cornish main,
  Oft didst thou, of thine own accord,
Stand forth to preach in accents plain,
  The Saviour Who is Christ the Lord.

HE took thee hence: whose latest breath
  To His eternal praise was given;—
So sure, so confident in death,
  That death was but the doors of Heaven;
God took thee hence: and pure and bright,
  Like metal in yon furnace tried,
Angels have welcomed in the height
  A soul whom God hath glorified.

W. C. B.

PENZANCE:
PRINTED BY BEARE AND SON,
21, MARKET PLACE.

CPSIA information can be obtained
at www.ICGtesting.com
Printed in the USA
BVHW09s1001200718
522186BV00018B/710/P